Chartered Banker Credit and Lending 2015/16

Published June 2015

ISBN 978 1 4727 2671 1

British Library Cataloguing-in-Publication Data
A catalogue record for this book is available from the British Library

Published by

BPP Learning Media Ltd,
BPP House, Aldine Place,
142-144 Uxbridge Road,
London W12 8AA

Printed in the United Kingdom by Ricoh UK Limited

Unit 2
Wells Place
Merstham
RH1 3LG

www.bpp.com/learningmedia

Your learning materials, published by BPP Learning Media Ltd, are printed on paper obtained from traceable sustainable sources.

Welcome to BPP Learning Media's Chartered Banker, Credit and Lending **Passcards**.

- Passcards **save you time**. Important topics are summarised for you.
- Passcards include **diagrams** to kick start your memory.
- Passcards follow the overall **structure** of the BPP Study Texts, but **Passcards** are not just a condensed book. Each card has been separately designed for clear presentation. Topics are self-contained and can be grasped visually.
- Passcards are **just the right size** for pockets, briefcases and bags.
- Passcards **focus on the exam** you will be facing.

Run through the complete set of **Passcards** as often as you can during your final revision period. The day before the exam, try to go through the **Passcards** again! You will be well on your way to passing your exam. **Good luck.**

1 : The Banker/Customer Relationship

Topic List

The banker/customer relationship is established when an account is opened and the first transaction passes through it. With a service, the relationship starts when the bank agrees to provide the service.

The law regarding appropriation of payments includes Clayton's case.

Death of a customer removes the banker's authority to pay out of funds and bankers need practical knowledge of the laws of testate and intestate succession.

Electronic funds transfer is an integral part of banking and the banker's duty of care in honouring a customer's cheques applies equally to electronic debits to the account.

Bank customers

Personal

Business

- Sole traders
- Partnerships
- Limited companies
- Others, eg clubs, associations, government

- Limited Partnership Act 1907
- Limited Liability Partnerships Act 2000
- Limited Liability Partnerships Regulations 2001

DEBTOR

CREDITOR

THE BANK

DEBTOR

CREDITOR

SAVINGS

LOAN

The relationship between the bank and the customer is that of debtor and creditor

The rights of a banker are

- To charge a reasonable commission for the bank's services
- To earn interest on loans
- To set-off
- To return unpaid any cheque (or debit on the account) which would create an unauthorised overdraft or which would exceed an agreed overdraft limit

A banker can use the principle of set-off where there are two accounts in the name of the same customer, one in debit and one in credit. Unless there is an express or implied agreement to the contrary, the banker can set-off the debit balance on one account against the credit balance on the other account by giving reasonable notice of his intention to do so

The duties of the banker are

- To receive money and collect cheques for the customer's account
- To honour customers' cheques
- To act in good faith and without negligence when dishonouring customers' cheques
- To inform the customer of any forgery of his/her signature
- To maintain secrecy regarding the affairs of customers
- To provide bankers' opinions when requested
- To give reasonable notice before closing a credit account

Provided

- That adequate cleared funds are available, or appropriate borrowing arrangements have been made
- That the cheques are in order technically
- That payment is demanded at the proper place and during business hours; and
- That there is no legal or other impediment preventing the banker making payment

It is the customer's duty

- To ensure that there are sufficient funds in the account, or a suitable overdraft has been arranged in advance
- To inform the bank if they know their signature has been forged
- To exercise reasonable care in drawing cheques
- To pay charges

Banking Conduct of Business Standards

Following the financial crisis of 2008, banks have moved away from the voluntary Banking Code and now comply with Financial Conduct Authority (FCA) regulation. The FCA have issued a **Banking Code of Conduct Sourcebook** (BCOBS) and also their **'Principles for Business'** (www.fsahandbook.info/FSA/htm/handbook/)

The British Bankers Association, the Building Societies Association and the Payments Council have issued an **'Industry Guidance for the FCA Banking Conduct of Business Sourcebook'** (BOCBS) (www.bcobs_ig_jan_2011_final[1].pdf)

The law regarding appropriation of payments was established almost 200 years ago in what is now known as the rule laid down in *Clayton's Case* (**Devaynes v Noble 1816**). The rule is that the first in/first out principle should apply in accordance with the dates of the transactions in the account.

Example 1: Current account – John Smith

		Dr £	Cr £	Balance £
April 1				Dr 500
April 3	Cash		200 (A)	Dr 300
April 4	Cash		300 (B)	Nil
April 8	Cheque	400		Dr 400
April 10	Cheque	500		Dr 900
April 12	Cash		400 (C)	Dr 500
April 16	Cheque	600		

The rule in *Clayton's Case* will operate as follows:

Item A partly extinguishes the opening £500 debit balance.

Item B totally extinguishes the opening £500 debit balance.

Item C extinguishes the debit entry of April 8.

The debit balance on April 12 is made up by the debit item on April 10.

Clayton's Case is an important one for bankers as it covers a situation that occurs many times in practice

Example 2: Betty Brown and Greg McPherson

Joint account (joint and several liability agreed)

		Dr £	Cr £	Balance £
April 1				Dr 500
April 3	Cash		200 (A)	Dr 300
April 4	Cash		300 (B)	Nil
April 8	Cheque	400		Dr 400
April 10	Cheque	500		Dr 900
April 12	Cash		400 (C)	Dr 500
April 16	Cheque	600		

The bank receives notification of Brown's death on May 11 but fails to stop the account.

Applying the rule of *Clayton's Case*:

- The credit entry on 12 May extinguishes part of the liability on Brown's estate.
- So, although the debit balance on 16 May is £1,100, Brown's estate is only liable for £500.
- The debit on 16 May constitutes new borrowing (£600) for which Brown's estate is not liable.

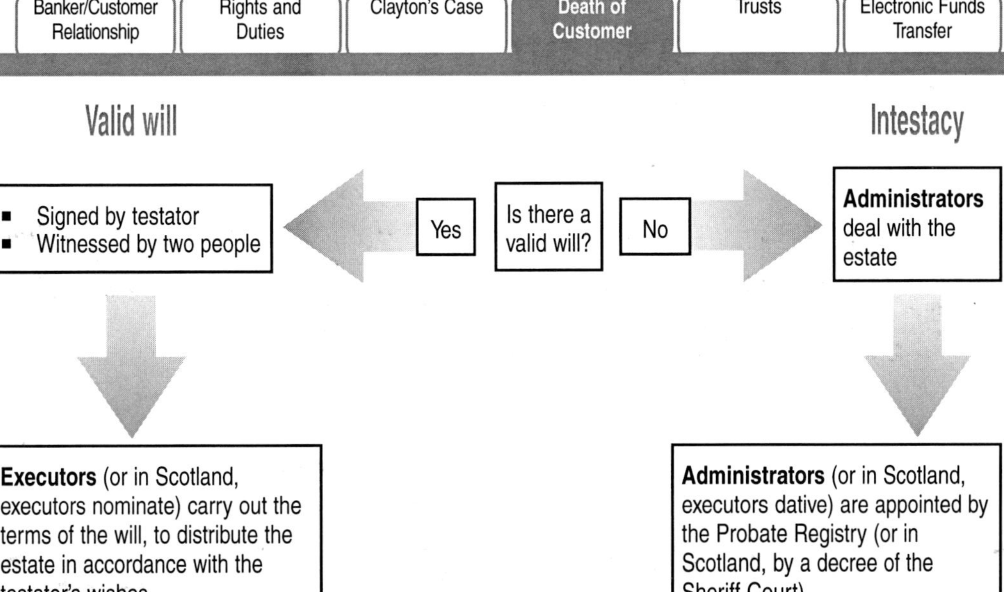
Valid will
Intestacy
■ Signed by testator
■ Witnessed by two people
Yes
Is there a valid will?
No
Administrators deal with the estate
Executors (or in Scotland, executors nominate) carry out the terms of the will, to distribute the estate in accordance with the testator's wishes
Administrators (or in Scotland, executors dative) are appointed by the Probate Registry (or in Scotland, by a decree of the Sheriff Court)

The banker's position after the death of a customer

An account in credit at the date of death

- Cheques presented should be returned 'Drawer Deceased' and all transactions on the account should be stopped
- The solicitors who are acting for the personal representatives should be told the position of the account and given a list of any documents or securities held on behalf of the deceased
- Details of probate or letters of administration should be recorded when presented to the bank
- Funds and securities can now be released to the personal representative(s)

An overdrawn account at the date of death

- Cheques presented should be returned 'Drawer Deceased' and all transactions on the account should be stopped
- A claim for the amount, plus interest, should be made to the solicitors acting in the winding up of the estate
- If a life policy has been assigned as security to the bank by the deceased, the bank will obtain a Death Certificate and arrange for collection of the proceeds. If there is a surplus after this is done, it should be held on deposit in the executor(s) (or administrator's) name until presentation of the probate or letters of administration

Law of succession

Intestate succession

Testate succession

Three conditions must exist before the rules of succession law apply:

- There must have been a death, the death registered and a Death Certificate granted to the person who registers the death
- The persons succeeding to the deceased's estate must survive the deceased
- The debts of the deceased must have been paid in full

The law of succession is laid down in England and Wales by the ***Administration of Estates Act 1925***.

In Scotland, there are prior and legal rights in the law of succession. Prior rights are granted to surviving spouses where there is no will. Legal rights apply to testate and intestate succession and cover the division of the deceased's estate among the surviving spouse and children.

A trust is an arrangement under which property is vested in one person for the benefit of another.

Three parties to a trust

- The testator (in Scotland the truster, or settlor) is the original owner of the property which is conveyed to the trustee to be held for the benefit of the beneficiary
- The trustee is the nominal owner of the trust property but is bound to administer it in accordance with the testator's directions
- The beneficiary is the person for whose benefit the trust exists

Classification of trusts

- An *inter vivos* trust is one which is set up while the testator is still alive
- A *mortis causa* trust is one which operates only on the testator's death, eg a donation made by the testator at the time of death to the beneficiaries in the trust
- A private trust is one where the beneficiaries are private individuals
- A public trust is one where the beneficiaries are members of the public, eg the trust sets up benefits to identifiable religious, educational, charitable or other public organizations or causes

Law of trusts is partly common law of contract.

Powers of trustees

- To sell the trust estate or part of it (in Scotland, also to grant feus and leases of heritable property)
- To borrow money on the security of real or personal property
- To purchase property for use as a residence for a beneficiary
- To appoint agents and solicitors and to pay suitable remuneration but only if required by the type of business required
- To grant all deeds necessary to effect their powers

Duties of trustees

- To gather and distribute the estate
- To exercise due care
- Not to delegate
- Not to be one who acts for own personal benefit
- To keep accounts
- To keep the funds properly invested (in a continuing trust)

Types of electronic funds transfers

- Bankers Automated Clearing Services (BACS) → Used for the payment of salaries, standing orders, direct debits and payments from businesses to their suppliers
- Electronic Funds Transfer at the Point of Sales (EFTPOS) → Used in the retail trade
- Clearing House Automated Payment System (CHAPS) → Used for sending same-day value sterling payments from one member bank to another
- Society for Worldwide Interbank Financial Telecommunication (SWIFT) → Used for carrying out cross-border electronic transfers

The duty of care owed by the banker to its customer applies equally when it comes to honouring debits made to the account electronically

2 : The Principles of Lending

Topic List

People/Character

Purpose/Amount

Repayment Capability/Terms

Security

Remuneration/Margin

Control of Lending

Under the basic rules of lending the following should be analysed:

- *A profile of the people/character*
- *That the purpose/amount meets your organisation's lending criteria*
- *Repayment capability/terms are consistent with cash flow projections and audited accounts*
- *Security which protects the bank and the customer*
- *Remuneration/margin to reflect the risk and the security provided*

No chapter on the principles of lending is complete without discussing how lending is controlled.

Preparation for a meeting to discuss a borrowing proposal

Existing customer

- How long have they been a customer of the bank?
- What is their reputation and track record?
- Have accounts been maintained in a satisfactory manner with previous borrowing repaid on time?
- Are there regular lodgements to the account?
- Are there any charges applied in respect of unauthorised overdrafts?
- Is there any evidence of items having to be returned unpaid for lack of funds?
- What are the figures for turnover (the business's sales), the maximum balance on the account, and the minimum and average balance figures over the last three years?)

Non-customer

- If an account is being transferred from another bank, ascertain the **reasons**

Reasons may include

- The customer is unhappy about poor service, high charges or the location of their current bank
- The borrowing proposal may have already been declined by their existing bank, or that the customer is seeking an alternative quotation for comparison purposes regarding pricing etc

Information gathering meetings should be held at your customer's business premises where possible; otherwise at least followed up with such visits

Useful mnemonics to ensure a uniform and consistent approach to lending:

CAMPARI	**C**haracter, **A**bility, **M**argin, **P**urpose, **A**mount, **R**epayment, **I**nsurance (security)
PARSERS	**P**erson (Character, Capacity, Commitment), **A**mount, **R**epayment, **S**ecurity, **E**xpediency, **R**emuneration, **S**ervices
PARTS	**P**urpose, **A**mount, **R**epayment, **T**erm, **S**ecurity
5 Cs	**C**haracter, **C**apacity, **C**apital, **C**onditions, **C**ollateral (security)

Obtain profile of the individual(s)

- Age
- Qualifications and experience
- Financial acumen
- Integrity and reliability
- Organisational ability and efficiency

Essential questions

- Has the borrower the experience and qualifications to make a success of the business?
- Can the customer keep within any borrowing limit agreed?
- Does the customer know volume of sales needed to make a profit?
- If goods are sold at a certain price, do they know how much it has cost to produce them and does this price also cover all the overheads and result in a profit?

Ascertain the character of the business

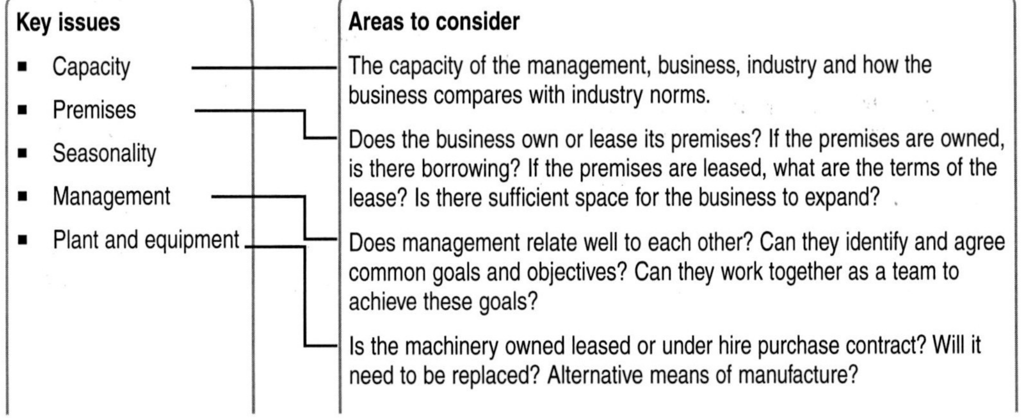

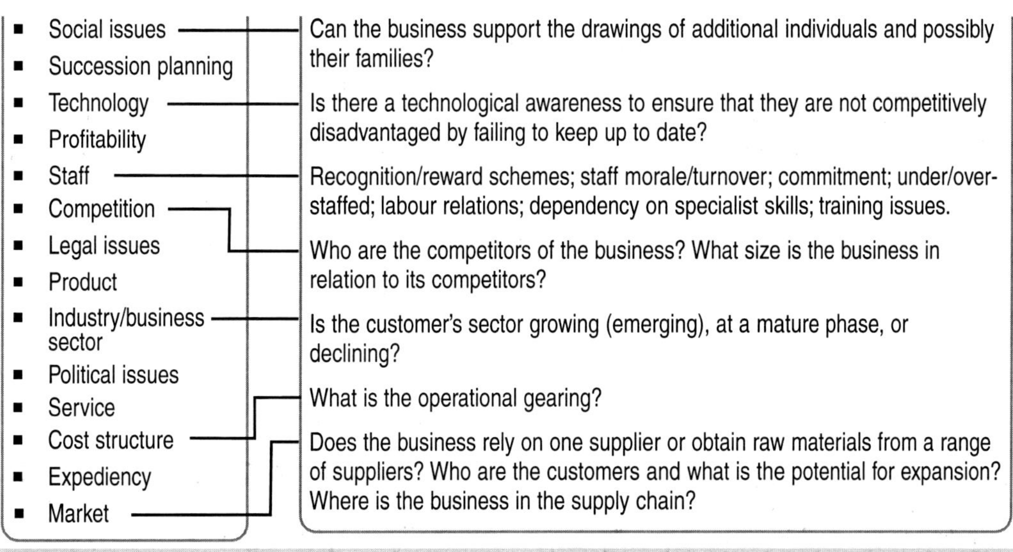
Social issues
Succession planning
Technology
Profitability
Staff
Competition
Legal issues
Product
Industry/business sector
Political issues
Service
Cost structure
Expediency
Market
Can the business support the drawings of additional individuals and possibly their families?
Is there a technological awareness to ensure that they are not competitively disadvantaged by failing to keep up to date?
Recognition/reward schemes; staff morale/turnover; commitment; under/over-staffed; labour relations; dependency on specialist skills; training issues.
Who are the competitors of the business? What size is the business in relation to its competitors?
Is the customer's sector growing (emerging), at a mature phase, or declining?
What is the operational gearing?
Does the business rely on one supplier or obtain raw materials from a range of suppliers? Who are the customers and what is the potential for expansion? Where is the business in the supply chain?

People/Character | **Purpose/Amount** | Repayment Capability/Terms | Security | Remuneration/ Margin | Control of Lending

Is the purpose of the loan legal?

Yes

Even if the purpose of the loan is legal, the following criteria must be met:

1. Your bank's own policy on lending to particular types of customer
2. Credit controls imposed by government or financial services regulators
3. Financial Conduct Authority guidelines applicable only in the UK

No

Be aware that some customers will be blatant and state that they want money for an illegal or unsuitable purposes. The bank's reputation would be at risk if money was lent to a customer liable to participate in such activities

Seven basic reasons why businesses borrow

1. To finance operating costs, variable costs, and fixed costs (such as wages, salaries, heat and light etc) until trade debtors are converted into cash

2. To finance stocks until they are converted to finished goods, sold and the debtors turned into cash

3. To finance the purchase or refurbishment of property, plant and equipment until they are used up over many trading cycles in producing output which is converted to sales and then to cash

4. To finance a whole range of assets, such as stock, debtors and fixed assets, and pay additional operating costs, etc, required to support rapid growth

5. To finance a change in the company's ownership, such as a management buyout

6. To finance one-off projects, such as property development

7. To finance survival until the company can be turned around. The business may be leaking cash, making insufficient profits, or incurring losses

Remember, customers may require borrowing for more than one purpose. Knowing what you are financing brings you closer to understanding your customer's business and its needs

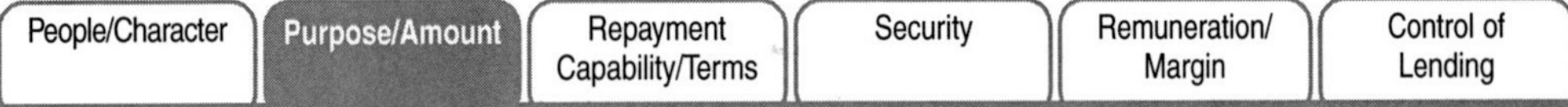

Example 1

A simple trading cycle of a newspaper street vendor, who operates totally in cash

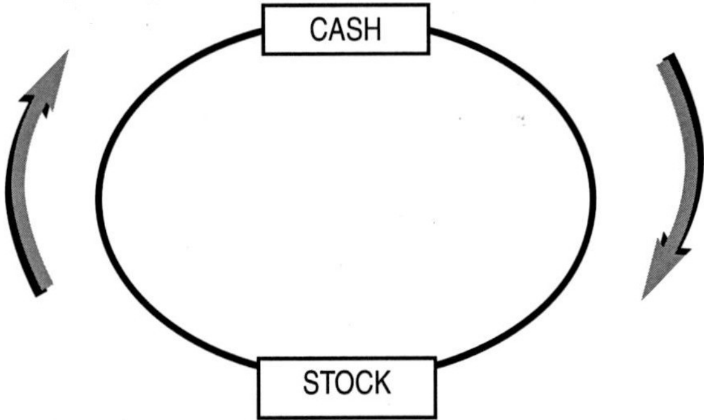

Example 2

A trading cycle for a manufacturing business

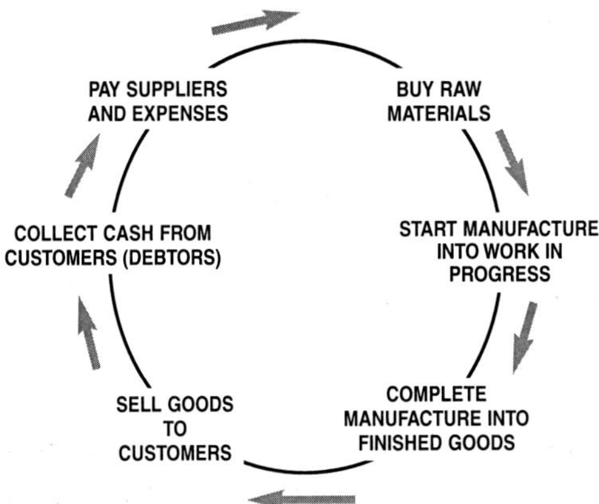

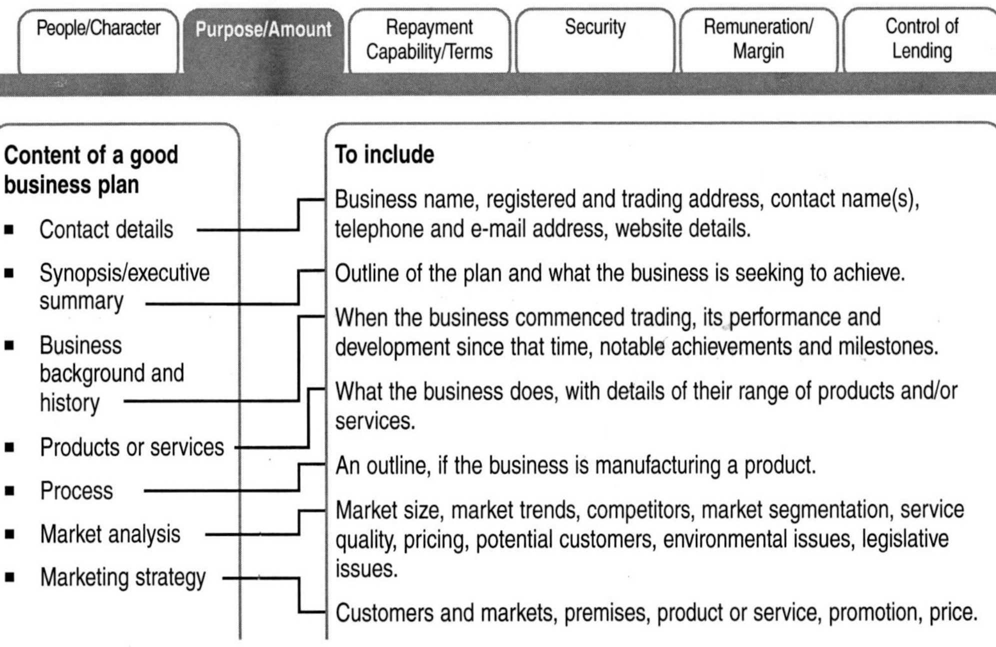
People/Character
Purpose/Amount
Repayment Capability/Terms
Security
Remuneration/ Margin
Control of Lending
Content of a good business plan
Contact details
Synopsis/executive summary
Business background and history
Products or services
Process
Market analysis
Marketing strategy
To include
Business name, registered and trading address, contact name(s), telephone and e-mail address, website details.
Outline of the plan and what the business is seeking to achieve.
When the business commenced trading, its performance and development since that time, notable achievements and milestones.
What the business does, with details of their range of products and/or services.
An outline, if the business is manufacturing a product.
Market size, market trends, competitors, market segmentation, service quality, pricing, potential customers, environmental issues, legislative issues.
Customers and markets, premises, product or service, promotion, price.

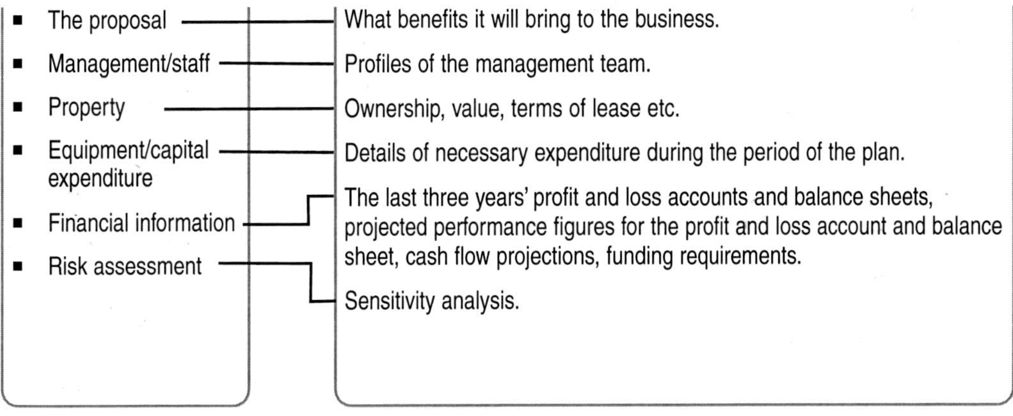
The proposal
Management/staff
Property
Equipment/capital expenditure
Financial information
Risk assessment
What benefits it will bring to the business.
Profiles of the management team.
Ownership, value, terms of lease etc.
Details of necessary expenditure during the period of the plan.
The last three years' profit and loss accounts and balance sheets, projected performance figures for the profit and loss account and balance sheet, cash flow projections, funding requirements.
Sensitivity analysis.

People/Character | Purpose/Amount | **Repayment capability/Terms** | Security | Remuneration/ Margin | Control of lending

Repayment capability

In any loan agreement the customer must be able to repay the loan in the agreed time span.

The customer must therefore be able to show, based on historical information and, more importantly, with projected figures, that the business can meet interest payments and repay the loan, with an adequate margin in case of the unexpected.

Projected, or budgeted, figures for income and expenditure, profit projections and cash flow analysis will form the basis of your assessment.

Terms

When you have established that the proposals are viable – that the business can make the proposed interest and loan repayments – then you work with your customer to determine the loan facility that best matches their **needs**

For capital expenditure, the term of the loan facility should normally tie in with the expected life of the asset purchased. Extra finance may be required for working capital to support the higher levels of debtors and stock during the working capital cycle

It may be appropriate to divide the total facility into an overdraft for working capital which will fluctuate and a term loan on which there is the discipline of fixed repayments

Security

It is always prudent to allow a margin for cover with the security taken, in case the security does not fetch the value attached to it when the loan was granted, eg the value of stocks and shares can fluctuate markedly

Typical items which can be used as security

- Legal mortgages over property (standard securities in Scotland)
- Floating charges (only from companies)
- Guarantees
- Life policies
- Stocks and shares

Covenants

The loan agreement may contain obligations on the borrower such as provision of information to the bank and adherence by the customer to financial covenants, such as interest cover maintenance, gearing levels and liquidity ratios

Any proposition should be able to stand on its own without the need for security

Remuneration

Generated from a number of sources:

- The difference between the interest rates charged to borrowers and that paid to depositors
- Loan arrangement fees
- Charges for the services provided by the bank, such as night safe facilities, etc
- Commission and payments received from outside agencies for referring clients, such as insurance commission

Margin

It is not unreasonable for the bank to charge a higher rate of interest when it considers that the risks are higher with a particular loan.

Similarly, a lower rate of interest may be applied to a fully secured loan to a customer with a strong performance track record.

At the time of writing, financial services regulators are examining the level of capital that a bank requires to hold to cover its credit and market risks. Higher levels of capital are sure to be required and this will bring increased pressure for adequate remuneration from bank lending and other services

To include

- Monitoring loan covenants
- Investigating **irregular balances**
- Involving all members of staff to obtain up-to-date and relevant information on a customer's affairs
- Undertaking visits to customer's premises
- Obtaining **additional sources of information**

Irregular balances

What is the reason for the irregularity on the account and what steps does the customer intend taking to put the matter right?

Are we prepared to formally approve the additional lending perhaps for a very short time or possibly over a longer period?

If we are not prepared to grant further advances, are we prepared to return the customer's cheques unpaid? Is this possible?

Additional sources of information

Stubbs Gazette
Local and daily newspapers
Dun and Bradstreet Registers
Extel cards
Information held at the company's office

Notes

3 : Credit Products and Services

Topic List

- Overdraft and Term Loans
- House Purchase Loans
- Personal Loans and Budget Account Loans
- Revolving Credit and Credit Cards
- Alternative Source of Finance

A sound knowledge of the credit products and services available is essential to match customer profiles to the appropriate credit product. Doing so leads to satisfied customers who are likely to stay loyal, use other bank products and recommend your bank to others.

Some of these products and services, like house purchase loans, personal loans, self-build finance and credit cards are available to personal customers, while others are used by businesses, although some individuals may have an overdraft and need a bridging loan when moving house, for example.

Overdrafts

- Offer a high degree of flexibility
- Only available on current accounts
- Repayable to the bank on demand
- Normally agreed subject to annual review
- Interest is only charged on the day-to-day balance outstanding on the account
- Are a convenient and inexpensive way of borrowing to cover a customer's short term requirements

Example 1

When a business customer buys stock, you would expect that the balance of the account would swing into overdraft and once the stock is sold and sales income received, the account should swing back into credit

Example 2

When a personal customer has an overdraft, the account may show a debit balance prior to the monthly salary being lodged to the account, when it will swing into credit again

When an account remains in debit permanently, this is referred to as hard core borrowing

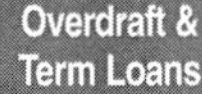

Terms loans

Variations on the theme of term loans, eg fixed rate loans, capped rate loans, discounted loans, commercial mortgages, professional practice loans

- Interest rates may be fixed or floating

Floating rates are more usual and fluctuate at a margin over bank base rate or LIBOR rate

- Drawdown of the loan may be in tranches, or instalments, on certain conditions being met
- Repayments are often geared to meet the cash flow of the business

There are 'holiday', 'bullet' and 'balloon' repayment schedules

- It is normal for security to be taken in support of term loans

Should the terms of the agreement be breached, the loan usually becomes repayable on demand, giving the bank the power to seek repayment and to realise its security

- Covenants are formal agreements made at the time of the loan

The loan agreement may contain obligations such as provision of information to the bank and adherence by the customer to financial covenants, eg interest cover, gearing and liquidity ratios

House purchase loans

The amount available to borrowers will often be a stipulated multiple of the customer's salary or a multiple of joint borrowers' combined salaries

As mortgage lending is covered in detail in Chapter 6, we will look at the following lending products:

- Bridging loans
- Self-build finance
- Equity/capital release loans

Bridging loan

- Required when a major purchase precedes a major sale
- Commonly encountered in house purchase and sale transactions
- In England and Wales the security is by way of a letter of undertaking
- It is normal for security to be taken in support of term loans
- In Scotland, the security is an assignation in security

Thus 'closed' bridging finance is a short term loan which will be repaid from a specific source

Business customers may need bridging finance for the purchase of new premises before the old ones have been sold, or when the customer is buying a new business prior to selling the present one

The letter of undertaking is issued by solicitors and addressed to the bank

The assignation in security is in the form of a letter from the customer, addressed to their solicitor, requesting that the free proceeds of the sale of the previous house are sent to the bank

In current market conditions open-ended bridging loans are not easy to agree

Equity/capital release loans

- Some banks are willing to lend customers a certain percentage of a customer's equity in the customer's property, provided the bank is granted security over the property
- The loans are normally granted at a rate linked to the banks mortgage rate
- The purposes of such loans are broadly similar to the purposes for personal loans

Self-build finance

A self-build loan is an advance that will finance the building, conversion or renovation of a property as the customer's **principal** residence

By the nature of the project, the funding for this type of borrowing must be flexible. Either option could be used:

- Funding of the project in arrears on confirmation of stage payments
- Funding of the project in advance may be considered depending upon the individual proposition, eg low LTV

The normal stages of a self-build project are:

- Completion of the foundations/underbuildings
- Delivery of kit – if the house is to be of a kit structure
- Erection of kit/wall plate level
- Building made wind and watertight
- Formation of rooms to plasterboard/roof tiles stage
- Final stage

It is normal practice to allow the customer to draw down at the end of each stage following formal certification from:

- A qualified architect
- A NHBC solo inspector/acceptable structural warranty inspector
- A structural engineer
- Some other suitably qualified professional

Personal loans

- Normally granted for the purpose of consumer purchases, eg cars, holidays and for home improvements
- Interest is charged at a flat rate, ie it is calculated on the total amount of the loan for the full term and applied to the amount of the loan at the commencement of the repayment term
- When an application is received it is usually credit scored to determine whether or not the bank is willing to grant the facility
- Personal loans fall within the 'regulated agreement' criteria as set out in the Consumer Credit Acts
- Some personal loans carry automatic life cover and there is an option for the customer to purchase accident, sickness and unemployment insurance

Budget account loans

- Enables customers to spread the cost of their regular bills and expenses over a year
- The customer adds up all the bills and expenses that are due over the course of the year and agrees the total amount with the bank
- The total is divided by twelve and this sum is paid in to the budget account by the customer each month from their operating account into which their salary is paid
- The customer may be issued with a separate cheque book with which to pay the bills, or they can arrange for their monthly and other direct debits/standing orders to be debited to the budget account

Revolving credit

- Allows a customer to draw up to a set limit, eg if a customer pays in £200 per month, the limit of borrowing may be set at £6,000 (30 × £200)
- Intended primarily for the professional type of customer with good income
- The application form is similar to that for a personal loan and the response data is credit scored
- It is usual to arrange for the monthly payment to be transferred from an operative account to the revolving credit account by standing order
- Interest is charged on a daily basis and normally applied monthly
- Insurance may be offered to pay off the debt in the event of the death of the customer or to meet repayments if the borrower has a prolonged illness or is made redundant

Credit cards

- The purchase of goods and services on credit subject to an agreed overall limit
- The issue of regular statements by the credit card company
- The option for the customer of either paying all of the sums due to the credit card company or electing to pay off only a portion of the sums due (minimum amount or 3 – 5%, whichever is the greater) and paying interest on the remainder

Showing:

- Their limit
- The transactions that have been made with the card(s)
- Any payments that have been received
- Any interest that has been debited to the account
- The current balance
- The amount of available credit remaining
- An estimate of the interest which will appear on the next statement based on the current balance

Company credit cards:

- An overall limit is agreed between the company and the bank and designated members of company staff are given a credit card with set limits within the overall agreed limit
- Statements are usually produced in respect of each cardholder with an additional summary statement showing the total amount due for payment from all cardholders
- Settlement of the sum due is normally effected by direct debit from the company's bank account

Hire purchase is an agreement to hire an asset with an option to purchase

Advantages for the customer of a hire purchase agreement:

- Small initial outlay
- Easy to arrange
- Certainty – the loan cannot be called in providing the terms are kept
- Availability when, for example, bank finance is not
- Fixed rate finance

Leasing is similar to hire purchase but the essential difference is that the lessee never becomes the owner

Two types of leases:

- Operating lease
- Finance lease

Continued

- Tax relief – interest payments are tax deductible and the asset may also be subject to a writing down allowance

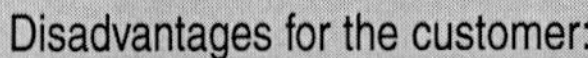

Disadvantages for the customer:

- More expensive than a cash purchase
- The fixed term means it may be impossible or expensive to make early termination

Advantages for the customer of a lease:

- Availability when, for example other sources are not
- Tax advantages, eg rental payments under an operating lease are tax deductible, as is interest under a finance lease
- The depreciation charge for a finance lease is tax allowable, dependent on the method of depreciation used and HMRC acceptability
- The obsolescence risk is transferred to the finance provider under an operating lease

Factoring is the raising of funds against the security of the company's debts

Factoring services:

- The factor will advance up to 80% of the value of debts immediately. When invoices are paid, the remaining 20%, less charges, is paid to the client
- The factor dispatches invoices and ensures that they are paid
- The factor provides insurance against bad debts

Available grant or loan support

- Regional Selective Assistance (RSA)
- DTI Grants for Innovation, Research and Development
- European Investment Fund (EIF)
- European Structural Funds
- Enterprise Finance Guarantee Scheme (EFG)

The government Business Link website (www.businesslink.gov.uk) provides wide-ranging information on grants and support schemes. As does www.bis.gov.uk

In Scotland, the Business Link website also has links to Scottish Enterprise (www.scottish-enterprise.com) and Highlands and Islands Enterprise (www.hie.co.uk)

Continued

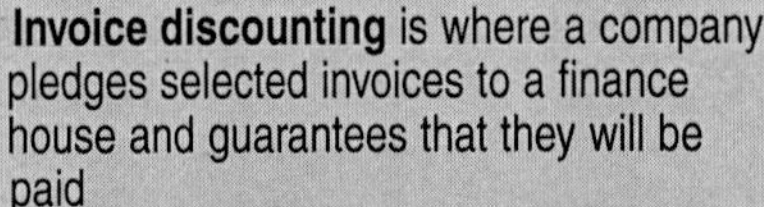

Invoice discounting is where a company pledges selected invoices to a finance house and guarantees that they will be paid

Franchising is the granting of a licence by one person (the franchisor) to another (the franchisee), which entitles the franchisee to trade under the trademark/trade name of the franchisor and to make use of an entire package, comprising all the elements necessary to establish a previously untrained person in the business and to run it with continual assistance on a predetermined basis

Benefits to the franchisee

- No need to come up with a new idea
- Well-established franchise operations will often have national advertising campaigns
- Good franchisors will offer comprehensive training programmes
- Assistance with determining the franchisee's financial requirements
- Details of competitors readily available
- Group discounts from suppliers
- Assistance with problem solving
- Management support to measure progress, celebrate success and plan for the future

Disadvantages to the franchisee

- Levels of success (or otherwise) can vary from sector to sector and from business to business
- Consideration needs to be given to the strength of the brand or image and whether it is transportable over a wide area
- The product or service needs to be adaptable to reflect any shift in market demand, eg McDonalds have tried to change both their perception and their menu to reflect heightened awareness of a healthy diet
- Franchising is a medium to long term investment and initially it still requires a sizeable amount of finance to cover start-up costs, fees, etc

Benefits to the franchisor

- Opportunity for a business with a proven product or service to sell, to expand rapidly without a prohibitive outlay of capital
- It can provide a broad distribution network and rapid market penetration
- High level of commitment from franchisees who have a stake in the business
- Benefit of the entrepreneurial skills which the franchisee can introduce, resulting in a better performance than otherwise might have been achieved

Disadvantages to the franchisor

- Major problems can arise if the franchisees are poorly chosen or become resentful of existing arrangements
- The franchisor needs to ensure that firm management and monitoring systems are established and maintained
- The franchisor has no share in the equity of the franchisee's business

Some example of franchises

- Avis
- The Body Shop International plc
- Prontaprint
- Spud U Like
- Thorntons

Equity finance

The raising of equity finance involves the owner giving up a share of their business in exchange for an investment in the business. Equity finance can be raised through business angels or venture capitalists

Business angels

Advantages

- Security is not usually required
- On average the investment is from three to six years, enabling the formulation of long term planning
- Often provide support in the form of expertise or network contacts

Disadvantages

- Dilution – the owner gives up part of the business and does not own 100% of the shares
- Proportion of the business profits goes to the investors

Venture capitalists

Advantages

- Security is not usually required provided there is an experienced management team with a solid, viable business plan
- Investment is usually for a period of three to ten years, enabling adoption of long term plans
- Often provide strategic input but do not usually get involved in the ongoing day-to-day management

Disadvantages

- Owner required to provide detailed information about the company
- Part of the ownership or control transfers to the venture capitalists

4 : Securities for Lending

Topic List

- Stocks and Shares
- Life Policies
- Guarantees
- Property/Heritage
- Securities from Limited Companies
- Other Forms of Security

Security is taken as an insurance, or protection, against things going wrong and the advance not being repaid. The bank takes security in case the cash flows needed to repay the loan do not materialise and the customer is unable to meet their obligations.

The future will always be uncertain and no matter how attractive and realistic a lending proposition may be, there is always a risk that what was anticipated does not happen.

The need for security is all the more necessary in the present times of financial volatility.

Advantages to a bank of taking shares as security

1. For quoted shares, it is a relatively simple matter to establish the current market value
2. A full legal title over most types of shares can be achieved
3. As a pledgee, under standard bank security clauses, it is only necessary for the banker to demand repayment and for the customer to default, before an immediate power of sale arises
4. Some shares are relatively stable to value, eg gilts which are nearing maturity
5. The formalities to complete the security are simple
6. A banker can acquire a good title even if bearer bonds are taken provided they are taken in good faith and for value, even if the pledgor's title is defective

Disadvantages to a bank of taking shares as security

1. Shares tend to fluctuate in value and, if the shares have to be realised at an unfavourable moment, the proceeds may realise far less than the bank anticipated
2. If the shares are unquoted, it is often difficult to obtain a valuation
3. The shares offered may be a director's qualification holding which could deprive the customer of his directorship
4. The Articles of Association of a private limited company may specify that a corporation, ie a bank nominee company, cannot be a registered holder of its shares
5. If a bank sends a transfer to a company for registration, and the transfer contains forged signatures, it is bound to indemnify the company even though it acted in good faith
6. The bank may at times rely on too narrow a spread of shares, eg one debt may be secured over shares in only two companies

Types of Shares

Registered securities (quoted, unquoted or on the unlisted securities market (USM))	These are the most common types of securities which are offered as security today and include ordinary shares, preference shares and debenture stock. To transfer the shares into the name of the bank's nominee company a stock transfer form must be completed and signed by the registered owner of the shares and sent with the share certificate (if one has been issued) to the company registrar
Bearer bonds	Bearer bonds are fully negotiable and as such it is normal to get the transferor to sign a memorandum of deposit or letter of pledge to confirm and outline the bank's rights
Hand-to-hand certificates	Hand-to-hand certificates may be described as quasi-negotiable and your organisation will have procedures for taking this type of security
British Government securities	Also referred to as gilt edged securities (or 'gilts'). The procedures are exactly the same as those for registered securities and the transfer form and certificate must be sent to the Bank of England as registrar
Unit trusts	Often described as 'open-ended funds'. If an impledgement is being taken, the certificate should be deposited with the bank and the renunciation form on the reverse of the certificate should be made in favour of the bank's nominee company. The certificate should then be submitted to the trustees, who will issue a fresh one, showing the nominee company as the registered holder
Investment trusts	Security over investment trust company shares is completed in the same way as for registered shares

Discounted values

1. Alternative investment market shares – generally around 25% of the value
2. FTSE shares – generally 50% of the value
3. Unquoted shares – generally no value due to their very limited marketability
4. Gilts – generally 75% of the value

It is important to have a share value monitoring system in place to value the security on a regular basis and to check this against the bank's exposure (or potential exposure) to ensure that an adequate margin is being maintained

Advantages of taking a life policy as security

1. The method of completing an assignment is simple
2. It is easy to establish the current surrender value of the life policy
3. If an assignation has been taken, it is a simple and quick matter to realise the security
4. As the assured pays more premiums, so the surrender value of the policy increases

Disadvantages of taking a life policy as security

1. A customer may be unwilling or unable to make regular premium payments
2. Contracts of life assurance are *uberrimae fidei* therefore if there has been any non-disclosure of a material fact, the contract will be voidable
3. There is a slight risk that the person who acts as proposer of the policy does not have an insurable interest in the assured
4. There may be a breach of the terms by the policy holder, thus making the policy voidable
5. If the policy was intended to benefit dependants upon the assured's death, and the policy is realised by the bank, bad publicity may result

5 The cost to the customer of taking this type of security is very low

6 If the assured dies, then the policy monies are immediately payable and the procedures for obtaining them are very simple

7 As further premiums are paid, so the bank's margin improves

8 The secondary market in endowment policies has established itself as a robust alternative to surrendering policies

Parties involved in a life policy

1. The **assurer**
2. The **proposer**
3. The **life assured**
4. The **beneficiary**

Taking the bank's security

In Scotland, security over a life policy is taken by way of an assignation, granted by the person to whom the policy belongs, in favour of the bank and its assignees. The form of assignation which banks use is known as an assignation in security. In England and Wales, banks use a Memorandum of Deposit

Types of policy

1. Endowment
2. Whole life
3. Term assurance
4. Unit linked

Endowment policies fall into four main categories:

1. Non profit
2. Full cost with profits
3. Low cost with profits
4. Unit linked endowments

When a life policy is received, it will be inspected to ensure that, if it is to be taken as security, the bank will be in a position to rely on the policy monies being payable to it, should it becomes necessary to realise the security.

The following factors must be considered:

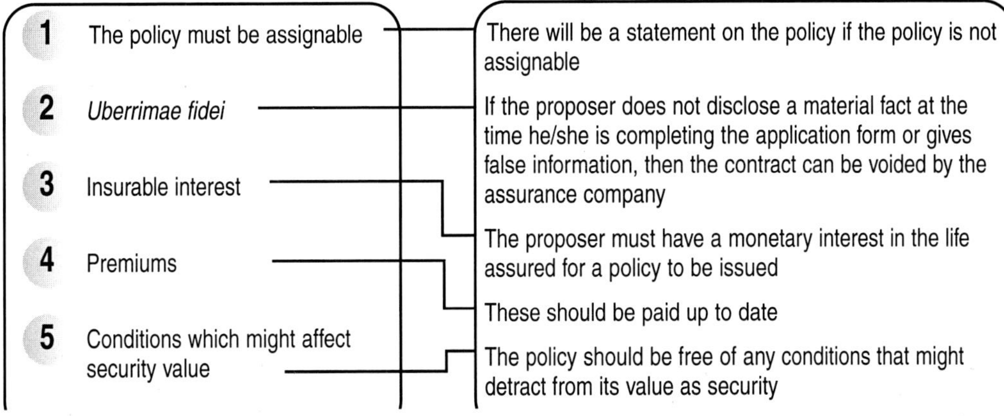

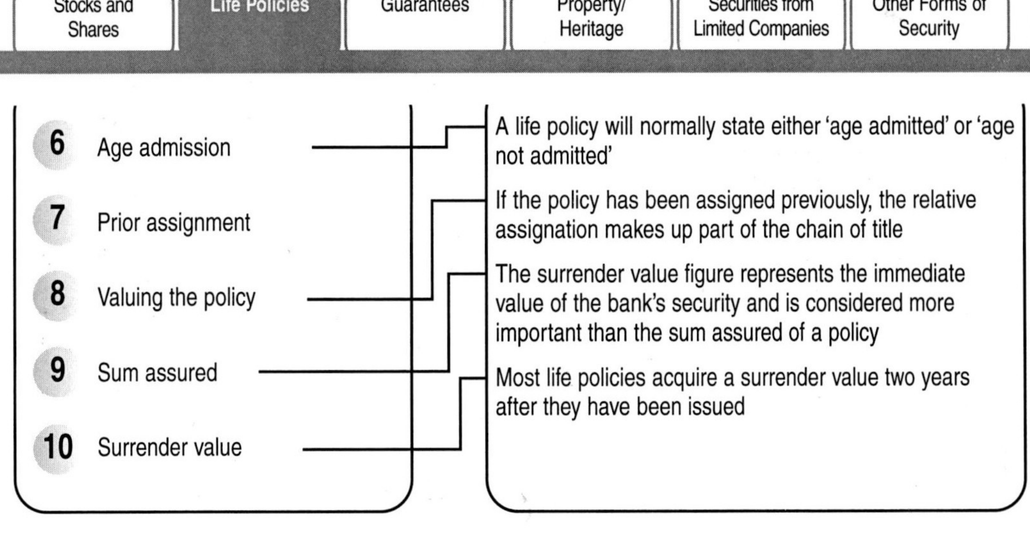
Stocks and Shares
Life Policies
Guarantees
Property/ Heritage
Securities from Limited Companies
Other Forms of Security
6 Age admission
7 Prior assignment
8 Valuing the policy
9 Sum assured
10 Surrender value
A life policy will normally state either 'age admitted' or 'age not admitted'
If the policy has been assigned previously, the relative assignation makes up part of the chain of title
The surrender value figure represents the immediate value of the bank's security and is considered more important than the sum assured of a policy
Most life policies acquire a surrender value two years after they have been issued

Advantages of using a guarantee as security

- Guarantees are easy to take, eg no form of registration necessary
- The far reaching clauses contained within a bank guarantee give the bank the maximum possible protection and powers
- The guarantor's maximum liability is fixed to the amount quoted on the form
- With the exception of a specific guarantee, all the principal debtor's liabilities are secured, now and in the future
- Provided the guarantor remains financially sound the guarantee has a stable value
- Where supporting security has been taken, which itself is stable in value, then the security is a very strong one
- Because guarantees are third party securities, they can be ignored when claiming against the principal debtor for recovery

Disadvantages of using a guarantee as security

- If the guarantee is not supported by security which has a stable value, the worth of the guarantee is entirely dependent upon the financial standing of the guarantor
- Although a guarantee contains many far-reaching clauses, a guarantor may still be able to avoid liability on a technicality
- It is often considered by the guarantor that the giving of a guarantee is a formality and that the liability is not a real one, which of course is not true
- If the guarantor will not pay up, legal action may be necessary which may be time consuming and expensive

Eight steps involved in completing the security

1	Establish the financial standing of the guarantor(s)	If a joint and several guarantee is being taken, an enquiry for the full amount is made on all the guarantors.
2	Review the general conditions	It is essential than an intending guarantor takes independent legal advice to prevent any undue influence claims.
3	Use the standard bank guarantee form	Where a guarantor suggests alterations, additions or deletions, reference will have to be made to the bank's legal department.
4	Place where the guarantee should be signed	Where independent legal advice is not taken, it is preferable to have all guarantees signed at the branch in the lending officer's presence.
5	Joint and several guarantees	The bank must ensure that when there is more than one guarantor, all sign, otherwise the security is unenforceable.
6	Correct specification of principal debtor	In normal circumstances a banker is expected to define correctly the name of the principal debtor.
7	Copy guarantee to guarantor(s)	If the guarantee is regulated by the Consumer Credit Act 1974 then each guarantor(s) should be provided with a completed and signed copy of the guarantee.
8	Annual status enquiry on guarantor	Annual status enquiries should be carried out on each guarantor.

The steps in taking a legal first mortgage in England and Wales are

1. Obtain the Title Information Document
2. Have it updated by sending to the Land Registry after obtaining the owner's consent
3. Search using form 94A and on receipt, note when the protection period for searching expires
4. Value the property
5. Search the local Land Charges Registry for any encumbrances such as road proposals, compulsory purchases, etc that might reduce the value
6. Check on overriding interests by asking the owner to complete a questionnaire and if any interests emerge, insist on independent legal advice and then they must postpone their interest

7. Execute the document of charge
8. Register at the Land Registry
9. Give notice to the property insurance company
10. Receive Title Information Document from the Land Registry

An equitable charge is obtained by taking the Certificate of Title to the property along with a signed Memorandum of Deposit

In Scotland security over land and property is not taken by means of a legal mortgage, but by way of a standard security.

Advantages to the lender of taking a standard security

- Generally, provided there are no problems with title to the property, the completion of this type of security is simple although solicitors have to be involved and the process can be time consuming and expensive
- The value of land and houses has historically been very stable and has tended to increase in value over a period of time, although in times of recession the value can fall

The various constituent parts of a standard security are:

- Personal obligation
- Description of the property
- Standard conditions
- Warrandice

Disadvantages to the lender of taking a standard security

- There is a risk that property may turn out to be difficult to sell either through deterioration in the upkeep of the property or lack of demand for the particular type of property in its area
- In realising its security the bank may have to consider evicting the occupants from the property if they will not vacate voluntarily
- In some cases the bank may require to enter into possession of tenanted property and have to take on the responsibilities of landlord
- As solicitors are employed to act for the grantor of the security and for the bank in constitution of the security, there are attendant legal expenses to be met by the customer
- Valuation can prove difficult and expensive

In England and Wales banks take a debenture as security. This incorporates a fixed and floating charge. In Scotland, banks take a Bond and Floating Charge.

Advantages

- The lender can take a charge over assets which would otherwise be difficult to charge
- The procedure is straightforward
- The lender can appoint an administrator following a petition to the court to grant an administration order

Charges granted by companies require to be registered in the register of charges either at **Companies House**, or in **Edinburgh** (for Scottish companies)

Disadvantages

- Valuing all the assets can be very difficult
- If the security has to be realised, the lender may find that certain assets have disappeared or have seriously fallen in value
- Creditors of a company sometimes feel that the execution of a floating charge signifies that the company is in financial difficulty
- If the security is to be realised, an administrator will have to be appointed whose costs will reduce the value of the assets being sold or disposed of
- The floating charge may not be valid if the business was insolvent when the security was granted

Other forms of security

Produce	The title of the goods is made over to the bank by way of the endorsement and delivery to the bank of a warehouse warrant or by means of a delivery order granted by the owner in favour of the bank and intimated to the storekeeper
Ships	The Merchant Shipping Act 1993 requires all UK vessels to be registered in Cardiff and as such allows banks to obtain an effective security
Assignation of contract monies and deeds	The right to payment of sums due, or to become due under a contract, is assignable unless there is a clause in the contract expressly stating that the debt cannot be assigned
Letters of Undertaking/ Irrevocable mandates	Most often seen in property transactions and where bridging finance is being provided against the sale proceeds of the property
Postponement of loan	Achieved by the lender, eg a director in the case of a director's loan, signing a letter of postponement
Cash lodgement	Such lodgements are usually provided by a third party, either direct or in support of a guarantee
Contingent liabilities	A contingent liability arises when a bank undertakes an obligation to a third party on behalf of a customer

Types of contingent liability

- Direct credit substitutes
- Transaction related
- Short term trade related
- Other, eg the bank may be asked to endorse a bill of exchange on behalf of a customer

5 : Financial Statements and How to Use Them

Topic List

- Financial Statements
- Ratio Analysis
- Cash Flow Reports
- Hard Core Borrowing
- Cash Flow Monitoring

Profit and Loss accounts, Balance Sheets and Cash Flow Statements are at the heart of business lending. These are the financial base documents that bankers analyse and from which a ratio analysis can be derived in order to establish trends within the business and highlight significant features. Ratios are also useful in comparisons with past results, peer performance, and industry norms.

Once an advance has been made, strict monitoring and control are required to ensure that the business is performing as planned and that the level of risk stays the same as was originally deemed acceptable. Prompt action will be needed to understand any deviation from the budgets agreed at the outset, and the appropriate action taken.

Audited accounts

Not all companies must have their accounts audited. The requirement is determined by the level of the sales turnover in the financial year, which is determined by the government. Companies with turnover of less than the threshold must have a Reporting Accountant's Certificate. The definition of a small or medium business and their legal requirements may change. They are available at www.companieshouse.gov.uk

Accounting standards

Accounting standards in the UK are developed by the Accounting Standards Board (ASB) and are contained in 'Financial Reporting Standards' (FRSs). The format and content of published accounts are governed by Financial Reporting Standard 3.

There is a trend now towards global standards for financial reporting. The IFRS Foundation is an independent, not-for-proft private sector organisation working in the public interest. Its principal objectives include developing a single set of high quality, understandable, enforceable and globally accepted international financial reporting standards (IFRSs) through its standard-setting body, the International Accounting Standards Board (IASB).

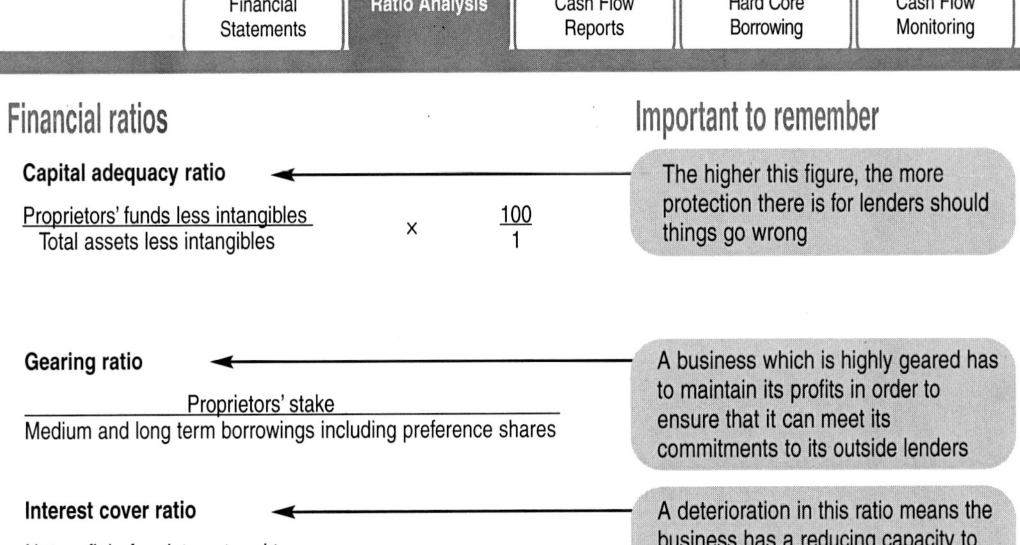

Financial ratios

Important to remember

Capital adequacy ratio

$$\frac{\text{Proprietors' funds less intangibles}}{\text{Total assets less intangibles}} \times \frac{100}{1}$$

The higher this figure, the more protection there is for lenders should things go wrong

Gearing ratio

$$\frac{\text{Proprietors' stake}}{\text{Medium and long term borrowings including preference shares}}$$

A business which is highly geared has to maintain its profits in order to ensure that it can meet its commitments to its outside lenders

Interest cover ratio

$$\frac{\text{Net profit before interest and tax}}{\text{Interest paid}}$$

A deterioration in this ratio means the business has a reducing capacity to meet the interest it has to pay

Liquidity ratios

Important to remember

Working capital ratio or current ratio

$$\frac{\text{Current Assets}}{\text{Current Liabilities}}$$

Gives an indication of the ability of a business to pay its short term debts as they fall due without having to resort to selling any fixed assets

Liquid ratio (or quick ratio/liquid asset ratio/acid test ratio

$$\frac{\text{Current Assets excluding Stock}}{\text{Current Liabilities}}$$

The usefulness of this ratio may depend on the proportion of stock in the current assets

Profitability ratios

Important to remember

Gross and net profit ratios

$$\frac{\text{Gross profit (or net profit)}}{\text{Sales}} \times \frac{100}{1}$$

Tells us whether the business is making a profit on its main area of activity, eg the buying and selling of products.

The net profit ratio is also an important measure of efficiency.

Return on capital employed

$$\frac{\text{Net profit}}{\text{Owners' stake}} \times \frac{100}{1}$$

It is essential to assess the total capital of the business including any long term loans put into the business by the owners and to deduct from this figure the intangible assets such as goodwill.

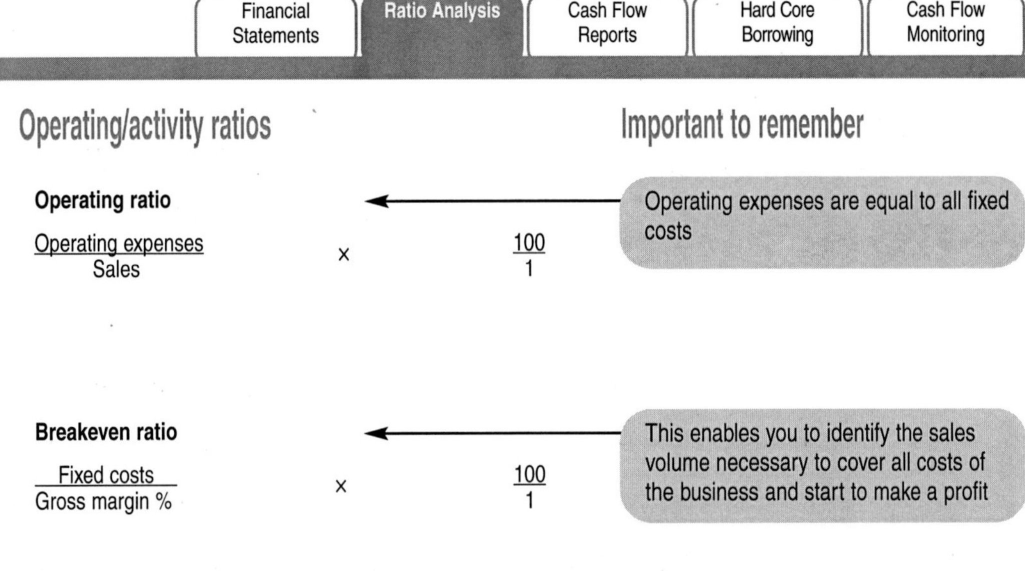
Financial Statements
Ratio Analysis
Cash Flow Reports
Hard Core Borrowing
Cash Flow Monitoring
Operating/activity ratios
Important to remember
Operating ratio
Operating expenses / Sales × 100/1
Operating expenses are equal to all fixed costs
Breakeven ratio
Fixed costs / Gross margin % × 100/1
This enables you to identify the sales volume necessary to cover all costs of the business and start to make a profit

Operating/activity ratios

Stock turnover ratio

$$\frac{\text{Cost of goods sold}}{\text{Average stock}}$$

$$\frac{\text{Year end stock}}{\text{cost of goods sold}} \times 365$$

Return on capital employed

$$\frac{\text{Debtors}}{\text{Credit sales}} \times \frac{365}{1} \qquad \frac{\text{Creditors}}{\text{Credit purchases}} \times \frac{365}{1}$$

Important to remember

Cost of goods sold = Opening stock + Net purchases – Closing stock

In the first equation we are looking at how long a period of credit is given to customers of the business. In the second, we are looking to see how much time is given to the business by its suppliers before their bills need to be paid

Cash flow reports enable us to assess our customers' ability to repay borrowed funds by taking the earnings of the business and adjusting them back to cash.

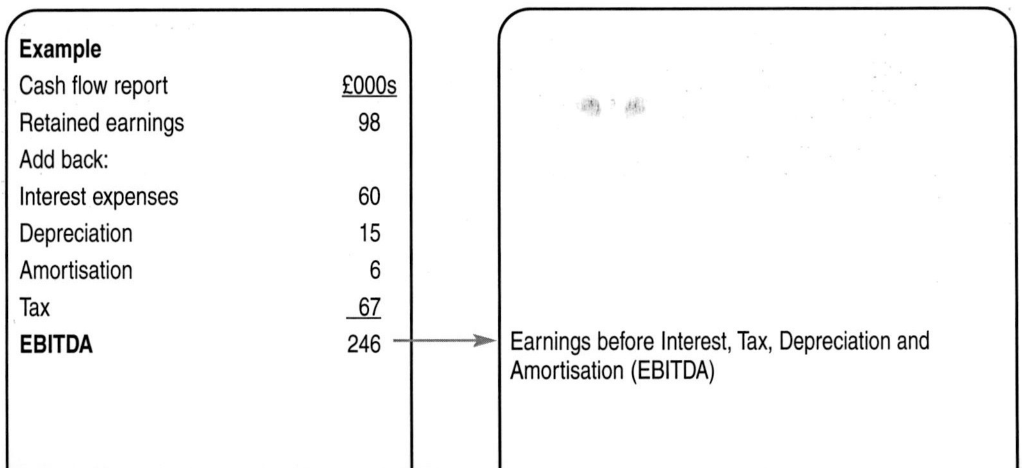

Example

Cash flow report	£000s
Retained earnings	98
Add back:	
Interest expenses	60
Depreciation	15
Amortisation	6
Tax	67
EBITDA	246

Changes in:	
Stock	(255)
Trade debtors	(52)
Trade creditors	348
Cash from operations	287
Finance costs:	
Interest expenses	(60)
CPLTD (prior year)	(20)
Total cash finance costs	(80)
Dividends paid	0
Capital expenditure	(33)
Cash after finance, tax and capital expenditure	148

Remember that:

- Increases in assets are a '(use)' of funds – profits are being tied up in stock or debtors
- Decreases in assets are a 'source' – funds are being released that were previously 'tied up'
- Increases in liabilities are a 'source' of funds
- Decreases in liabilities are a '(use)' of funds

Short term debt

Cash	(18)
Overdraft	(131)
CPLTD (current year)	25
Change in long term debt	(24)
	(148)

Current portion of long term debt (CPLTD)

The surplus of cash after finance, tax and capital expenditure of £148,000 has given the business a cash surplus which they have used to:

- Increase their cash on hand/at bank balance – the reason can be established if you talk to the customer
- Reduce the overdraft – was this voluntary or as a result of pressure?
- The CPLTD and change in long term debt are part of the normal debt repayment schedule; this should not change significantly unless the agreed term of repayment was varied at the customer's request

Overtrading arises from thee serious managerial mistakes

1 Initial under-capitalisation	The business has not raised enough capital/shareholders' funds to finance the anticipated level of trading
2 Over expansion	The business expands to such a degree that the capital base is insufficient to support the new level of activity
3 Poor utilisation of working capital resources	This may occur when planned profits and cash flow forecasts are not met and finite debt capacity is used up to replace lost profits instead of being used as planned to invest in working capital

Signs of overtrading include

- A progressive fall in the debtors/creditors ratios: this can be one of the earliest signs and happens when creditors increase more rapidly or fall more slowly than debtors
- Despite no increase in turnover, there are frequent requests to increase bank borrowing; increasing creditors and stock may be the reason
- A fall in the working capital ratio: this can indicate an increase in business without a corresponding increase in working capital
- In the early stages, gross profit may be maintained but there is a steady decline in net profit due to increasing expenses. In the later stages gross profit will also fall

Signs of overtrading in the bank account could be

- Increased incidence of irregular positions; requests to exceed the limit in anticipation of monies that are 'certain to come in'
- A reduction in the level of fluctuations between the maximum and minimum balances on a monthly basis
- Regular requests to assist with wages
- Monthly accounts being paid progressively later in the month
- Cheques to suppliers in round amounts, suggesting payments to appease them

The obvious way to avoid overtrading is for businesses to scale back the level of trading, ie to 'live within its means'

Other possibilities are

- Injection of capital – this can be new share capital, a long term loan, or injection of capital by a new partner – the drawbacks to this option can be a dilution of control of the business or higher interest costs
- Maintain tight control of working capital
- Lease of assets rather than outright purchase
- Buy fixed assets on hire purchase – this has the same impact as leasing but they end up owning the asset
- Reduce drawings from the business or don't pay a dividend
- Cut costs or improve efficiency

Cash flow monitoring includes

- Preparation of a cash budget
- Relating items of income to expenditure
- Interpretation of a cash budget
- Making comparisons between forecasted and actual figures
- Stock, debtor and creditor controls

If the cash flow is already completed, can the customer convince you that the figures are not only accurate but also realistic and achievable?

So much depends on the income forecast being generated. Therefore, you must be satisfied that the basic assumptions of income and expenditure are realistic. How does the customer justify the assumptions?

Interpretation of the cash budget leads us naturally to the key cash generating areas of the balance sheet – the working capital

If variances from projected figures are identified at an early stage, this enables you to work with your customer to address the situation and agree and adopt appropriate remedial action to avoid it becoming a bigger problem

Another key set of assumptions in any cash flow is about the terms of trade for the business. How long a period of credit will the business take from its suppliers? Do the figures show payment being made within the timescale agreed? Similarly, what collection period is used in the cash flow for the business's debtors? Are these terms of trade in line with the industry norm?

Example

Where the overdraft is gradually getting out of line with what was projected, the customer might agree to tighten debt collection procedures, thereby reducing the dependency on overdraft

6 : Credit Risk Practices for Retail Banking

Topic List

- Risk Management Framework
- Credit Scoring
- Money Laundering
- Mortgage Lending
- High Net Worth Customers
- Credit Risk Analysis

The different aspects of credit risk practices within the head office functions of banks and how credit risk fits within the overall risk management framework is examined in this chapter.

Credit scoring is an important decision making tool in lending to individuals and also with some SME lending. Credit reference agencies are an integral piece of the 'jigsaw' that comes together to form a credit decision.

A large part of bank lending is mortgages and there is a section on this important topic.

Finally, credit risk analysis pulls everything together and includes the assessment techniques used.

Risk

is defined as 'the possibility of incurring a misfortune or a loss'

With risk, including credit risk, there are three principal steps:

1. Understand what events could happen
2. Assess the likelihood of that event actually happening
3. Understand the impacts if the event did happen and what could be done to prevent loss either by avoiding the risk or by having a contingency plan in place to minimise any loss

The typical risk management model will include three lines of defence for a bank

1. The first line of defence will typically be front line bankers, treasury department, etc, made up of the bank's own personnel
2. The second line of defence will be policies and procedures, internal audit, credit approval, distressed lending units, group legal, operational risk, executive committees, etc, again mainly staffed by the bank's own personnel
3. The third line of defence will be the Board of Directors, the External Auditor, the Financial Services Authority, Government legislation, etc, this time with external personnel who will have contact with the bank's staff

The primary function of risk management is to

- Identify the issue(s) – understand what could happen
- Identify the likelihood – probability
- Put plans in place to solve or mitigate – plan
- Make sure the outcome is dealt with quickly – action/monitor

A bank will typically have a set number of committees which will address the following risk areas

- Credit risk ← The main activities that a Credit Risk Committee undertakes are:
- Asset and liability risk
- Market risk
- Insurance and investment risk
- Operational risk
- Legal and regulatory risk
- Strategy risk
- Audit

The main activities that a Credit Risk Committee undertakes are:

- Recommending the risk appetite and the direction (eg for certain industries)
- Regulatory adherence
- Maintaining and approving credit policies
- Portfolio management and credit quality
- Agreeing and monitoring risk and pricing models
- Lending authority control

Credit Scoring

Is the term used to describe systems within banks and financial institutions which allow lenders to automate their credit decision making while also managing the credit risk of those decisions. Credit scoring consists of a statistically derived model (the credit scorecard) which is used to predict a specific outcome and a set of strategies which drive the decision-making process

Application Scoring

In the credit risk arena, a number of different models can be used to predict different outcomes. For example, an application scoring model may be built to:

- Predict the likelihood of a new loan account going 'bad' or becoming delinquent
- Determine the amount of credit limit to be allocated to a new credit card

Behavioural Scoring

Behavioural scoring can be used to:

- Increase a credit card limit for an existing credit card customer
- Decide whether to pay or return transactions presented against an existing current account if insufficient funds are available

The scorecard refers to the set of points used in scoring an application. Points are allocated according to the characteristics of various applicants whose accounts:

- Were fully repaid in time with no issues
- Are then compared with the characteristics of those facilities that were either slow to repay and
- Are compared again, this time with those who did not repay their loan in full

- Predict the credit risk of approving a new current account and providing overdraft facilities

Application scoring is used for new and existing customers and is a single point in time assessment for credit

- Upgrade credit or debit cards from standard to gold and beyond

Behavioural scoring, unlike application scoring is used for existing customers only and is an ongoing, updateable assessment for credit

Benefits of credit scoring

- A consistent and impartial assessment of customers – all customers are treated the same and fairly
- Allows management to control the 'credit tap', that is, increase or reduce credit exposures, thus giving the bank control over approved volumes/'bad' rates
- A uniform method of processing standard customer requests
- An increase in ability to consider volume credit approvals irrespective of value
- Much improved management information systems – it is all electronic based
- An efficient, cost-effective method of credit risk assessment
- With a standard and tested system, the quality of the credit portfolio will be reliable during a stable economic cycle

Boundaries of credit scoring solutions

- A sizeable number of historical applicants and repayment patterns data are normally required to build a credit scorecard
- Can be expensive to build and put in place, although there is a choice between in-house built systems and off-the-shelf purchased systems
- Is time sensitive – efficiency deteriorates over time. Very old data can prove to be unreliable for making plans for tomorrow, so scoring systems need to be replaced or updated over time
- Is not infallible and errors can occur
- Not all lending decisions are suitable for a scoring solution
- Will not solve all credit issues

Monitoring credit scoring

Scorecards are regularly reviewed to ensure that they are still appropriate to the customer base of the financial organisation. The review will normally measure the following performance areas:

- Stability of the current score in comparison with the historical performance – has the level of declined applications increased, for example?
- Have there been changes to the makeup of the customer base?
- How effective has the override performance been (where the lender has not followed the course of action recommended by the scoring system) – has there been stability in override decisions?
- Has the predictability of the level of defaults or approvals matched actual results?

Organisations affected by or who use credit scoring

- Association for Payment Clearing Services (APACS)
- British Bankers Association (BBA)
- Building Societies Association
- Consumer Credit Trade Association
- Council for Mortgage Lenders
- Credit Card Research Group
- Finance and Leasing Association
- Mail Order Traders Association

Credit reference agencies (CRAs)

The information held by a CRA falls into two separate areas:

Public Information

Sourced from:

- UK Electoral Roll maintained by local authorities
- County court judgements, Scottish decrees and Northern Ireland enforcements
- Sequestrations, trust deeds, bankruptcies, individual voluntary arrangements and administrative orders

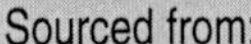

Shared credit account information

Sourced from:

- Experian Ltd
- Equifax plc
- Callcredit plc

Money laundering regulations affect

- All banks, building societies and other credit institutions that accept deposits and offer lending and leasing
- All individuals and firms engaging in investment business within the meaning of the Financial Services Act 1986
- All insurance companies covered by the European Life Directives, including the life business of Lloyd's of London
- Bureaux de Change, cheque encashment facilities, and money transmission services, etc

The regulations require that financial institutions

- Ask new customers to prove their identity
- Check sources of any one-off transactions exceeding £10,000
- Check the sources of separate or linked transactions over £10,000
- Keep adequate records showing evidence of the customer's identity and transactions for five years
- Maintain internal reporting procedures with one member of staff responsible for receiving reports of suspicious transactions who should inform and cooperate with the police

Breach of these regulations can result in imprisonment and/or a fine

Two significant risks in relation to mortgage lending

Repayment risk – ability of the customer to meet future payments

Property risk – value of the house itself and quality of the registered title

Other factors which come into the assessment of a mortgage application are:

- Conduct of accounts
- Evidence of savings
- Income and expenditure profile
- Conduct of previous mortgage or tenancy agreement
- Previous credit history
- Employment and salary

A lot of information is required to assess ability to repay and to see that the risk is acceptable:

- The level of borrowing and loan-to-value
- The level of contribution from the applicant and its availability
- The term of the loan
- The property and its condition (including any restrictions of title)
- Creditworthiness of the applicant

For high net worth customers credit scoring may not arrive at a satisfactory credit risk assessment as their asset base and income is substantially above either the national or average for the typical bank, so that a manual assessment may be required in addition. Financial analysis can be carried out by consulting information about the customer's assets and liabilities and their income and expenditure.

When analysing the Statement of Net Worth you should:

- Establish the assets and liabilities of the customer
- Confirm their accuracy in both value and ownership
- Assess the liquidity risk – the current ratio and quick ratio
- Assess appropriateness of the debt structure
- Assess the likelihood of contingents crystallising

The Statement of Assets and Liabilities is a useful prompt for further questions. For example:

- Property asset details will allow you to establish income streams from rented properties and allow you to check on the servicing costs to ensure that they are included in the customer's expenses
- Income from rented properties should be net of estate agent's or letting agent's fees, and tax
- You will be able to establish if the customer is allowing for rental voids during the year
- Ascertain if there are any assets free of mortgages which could be available as security if you feel it is needed
- Expiry of credit facilities at your bank or another competitor can alert you to an imminent and potential new borrowing need of your customer

The same principles of lending (as in Chapter 2) apply to lending to personal customers, including high net worth personal customers.

A mnemonic like the '5 Ps of credit' may help

Person

- Is your customer trustworthy? If not stop your analysis at this point and do not commit to lending
- Does the credit risk at the macro and overall levels appear logical, reasonable and make sense?
- Does the customer's profile fit with your own bank's strategic and marketing objectives?
- Is your customer nearing retirement or do they have a young family which may explain the lack of elasticity in the surplus of income less expenditure?
- What industry sector is the customer employed in? Is it stable or vulnerable to economic downturns?
- What is the net worth surplus percentage? Do they have high or low gearing or leverage?

Purpose

- Is the purpose for which the credit facilities are being granted legal and within your bank's credit policy?
- Regarding legal risk, you need to ensure that the documentation for the credit facilities and for any security provides a legal and binding contract
- Is the borrowing properly structured?
- Is there a logical fit between the purpose for which the asset is being financed and the source of repayment?

Payment

- A major part of credit risk assessment is making sure that the interest cost can be met and repayments made as arranged
- Having the income to repay you mandated to the bank is a comfort
- The primary source for servicing the borrowing and meeting loan payments is usually from the surplus of income over expenditure

Protection

This comes initially from the income and assets of the customer. If these do not repay you, then you may need to resort to the security held

- The risk can be mitigated by setting formal triggers (covenants, or agreements) in the loan documentation
- Have you satisfactorily covered the external market risks?
- Insurance is used to mitigate an unforeseen event and the aim is to cover the customer personally and their assets
- Have arrangements been made to regularly review the facilities during their lifetime to meet audit risk requirements?
- Are insurance policies still in place, adequate to cover the assets and have premiums been paid?

Premium

- What is the credit risk/reward ratio? Are you charging sufficient in interest to cover the credit risk your bank is being asked to take?
- Your bank may have a pricing model that will assist you in establishing the hurdle interest rate and arrangement fee to be charged for the facilities
- You will recall that a bank must manage its return on capital employed to ensure that adequate returns are made to meet its costs and provide the returns shareholders expect

Notes

7 : Credit Risk Practices for Business Banking

Topic List

Risk Management Strategy

Market or Industry Risk Assessment

Business Risk Assessment

Financial Risk Assessment

Documentation and Pricing for Risk

All businesses represent a credit risk; no matter their size, legal structure, number of employees, whether in a developing, mature or declining industry sector, high or low tech, growing or downsizing, etc. For this reason, any business will be subjected to some sort of credit risk analysis. The level and depth of the credit analysis will depend on a number of factors, normally linked to the strategic direction and objectives of the bank, and the size of the exposure.

All lending involves risk. It is the banker's duty to assess and manage these risks, deciding which risks to accept and which to reject. Management of risk is at the core of banking.

Using a risk management strategy as a template to manage the credit risks, we need to:

- Identify the issue(s) – understand what could happen
- Identify the likelihood – probability
- Put plans in place to solve or mitigate – plan
- Make sure the outcome is dealt with quickly – action/monitor

To carry out an analysis and assessment, the following areas need to be examined:

- Market or industry risk assessment
- Business risk assessment
- Financial risk assessment
- Documentation and pricing for risk

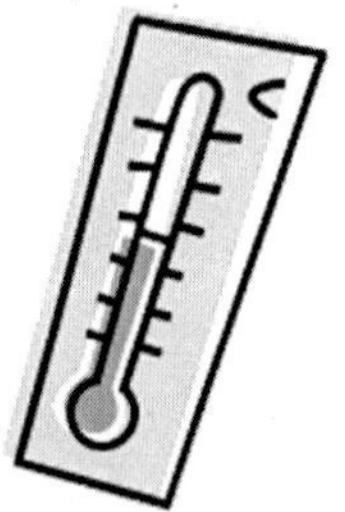

Three degrees of risk

1. Low risks which perhaps we do not require to mitigate
2. Moderate risks which should be mitigated
3. High risks which really must be mitigated otherwise the probability of loss is too great

Economic condition

Low risk – This applies where there is stable or slow growth in the economy

Moderate risk – This applies where there is rapid growth or moderate levels of inflation in the economy

High risk – A downturn in economic activity is evidenced by two or more consecutive quarterly declines in Gross Domestic Product (GDP) or other key indicators, such as high unemployment rates or high rates of inflation

Scale of seasonality

Low risk – The majority of earnings are generated evenly during a twelve month trading period

Moderate risk – Income in one quarter may be generally higher than in any of the three remaining quarters in a twelve month trading period

High risk – Income in one quarter accounts for more than 50% of the total income for a year during a trading year

Industry cycle comparative to economy

Low risk – The industry cycle is unaffected by what is happening in the economy and can therefore be regarded as independent

Moderate risk – The industry cycle moves in a converse pattern to that of the economy and therefore is regarded as counter-cyclical

High risk – The industry cycle moves parallel with that of the economy (concurrent); or the industry cycle preceded economic recovery or slowdown (leading); or the industry cycle follows with a time gap any economic recovery or slowdown (lagging)

Industry profitability

Low risk – Typically, net margin (NM %) will be low and profitability moves very little during economic downturns

Moderate risk – Typically, NM % will be stable and will suffer a moderate reduction in profitability during economic downturns

High risk – Typically, profitability will be high during expansionary periods and loss making during economic downturns. NM % will fluctuate dramatically

Industry product cycle

Low risk – Products or services are fairly standard; there is a degree of oversupply in the market; real prices are falling, and lower profits are being seen. The industry is generally considered to be mature

Moderate risk – The market for the products or services continues to grow and improvements to design are necessary, ie maturing

High risk – Emerging businesses will have been recently established as a result of demand changes for products and services in their markets. Declining business is characterised by mass produced products or services, lowering prices and profitability

Degree of overcapacity in the market

Low risk – This is characterised by a minor overcapacity of demand in the market. It is displaying demand that is exceeding the supplies available for the industry's products

Moderate risk – Demand and supply and production are balanced

High risk – There is significant overcapacity in the industry and demand from consumers is not keeping up with what the industry is producing

Cost structure

Low risk – More variable costs

Moderate risk – Balanced variable and fixed costs

High risk – More fixed costs than variable costs

Barriers to exit

Low risk – Assets can be easily liquidated or the business can be sold within a short space of time

Moderate risk – Due to the specialised nature of the business's assets, a buyer of the assets or the entire business would probably be a player already active in the industry; or there could be political influences that restrict realisation of the assets/business

High risk – Significant high costs of realising the assets of the business exist; there could be union agreements in place regarding redundancy or closure terms; strategic alliances with other businesses may prevent exit due to the penalties that would require to be paid, or simply because all the other players in the market are in a similar situation and there is a lack of willing buyers

Strength of domestic competition

Low risk – The business is part of an oligopoly or monopoly

Moderate risk – As a result of brand loyalty, the business is minimally threatened by competitors who produce similar products

High risk – The business has a product that is standard, readily available elsewhere and is subject to product substitution; or the loss of market share is a constant worry. Domestic competition is considered substantial

Strength of foreign competition

Low risk – As the industry or its products are new, foreign imports are not yet a danger

Moderate risk – Due to customer demand, there is insufficient volume to keep pace with this need domestically and this allows competitively priced foreign imports to enter the home supply chain

High risk – The business has a product that is standard and is readily available from overseas competitors at a cheaper price

Sales – customer/industry concentrated

Low risk – Sales are well spread to many customers across many markets or industries

Moderate risk – There are pockets of concentration of sales to individual customers or markets/industries that make up more than say, 25% of turnover

High risk – Sales are concentrated on a few customers or markets/industries that make up more than 50% of turnover

Threat of substitutes

Low risk – The threat from substitute products or services is insignificant, low or even remote, due to strong customer brand loyalty or the patents or licences the company holds for its products

Moderate risk – There are some substitutes available, but they have not made an impact on demand for existing company products due to their superior quality or brand loyalty or their reputation

High risk – Substitute products are widely available from different industries and competition has created falling prices, or products of the same or better quality can be obtained elsewhere and there is generally no brand loyalty

Bargaining power of buyers

Low risk – Consumers cannot influence the price of goods or services due to limited supply or the dearth of alternatives

Moderate risk – Consumers may be able to influence selling price to a limited extent, but generally the businesses within the industry can control prices

High risk – Selling prices of products and services must be competitive due to their general profile and availability of alternatives

Bargaining power of suppliers

Low risk – Suppliers have little or no ability to influence the price of goods or services due to availability of alternatives

Moderate risk – Suppliers can have some influence on the prices they charge the business for materials and suppliers

High risk – Suppliers have considerable influence over the prices of their goods or services due to limited supply or lack of alternatives

Barriers to entry

Low risk – Start-up costs are insignificant with merchandise not easily differentiated and this allows ease of entry into the market

Moderate risk – Some level of capital investment is needed and access to distribution channels is necessary before new entrants may begin making sales

High risk – Significant barriers exist because of brand name loyalty, high capital investment requirements, or there is limited access to distribution channels and any of these makes entry into the industry difficult

Degree of outside regulation

Low risk – There are few, if any, government laws/regulations affecting the industry. The industry could be self-regulating

Moderate risk – There are some government laws/regulations affecting the industry. On the whole the industry is self-regulating

High risk – The industry operates in an environment which is highly controlled by government laws/regulators

Economic cycle success

Low risk – Both long and short term market disturbances are dealt with in an effective and efficient manner. Management reacts quickly and appropriately to adverse cyclical/seasonal trends and, as a result, maintains consistent profitability and cash flow

Moderate risk – The business has been able to absorb short term market disturbances including economic or business swings. However, longer term disturbances could adversely affect the business's creditworthiness

Business life cycle

Low risk – The business will be classed as mature where goods or services are provided in a standard format and do not really change. Competition will be intense and gaining market share will be difficult

Moderate risk – The business is growing, providing goods or services that are better than those provided by their competitors. This allows them to charge a premium which should result in a higher profit

High risk – Declining businesses will be characterised generally by goods or services which are nearly identical to those of their competitors and customer demand is falling

Suitability of company product to market

Low risk – The products are regarded as staple items for survival such as food, heat, water

Moderate risk – Typically these will be purchases that can be deferred, if cash flow becomes tight

High risk – These products will be considered luxuries, there will often be cheaper alternatives but they will not have the same *cachet* as the 'real thing'

Supply chain risks

Low risk – There is no limitation of suppliers; the raw materials and other inputs can be sourced locally; there is no perceived shortage in the next 12 months and there is sufficient reliable transport readily available

Moderate risk – There is some shortage of suppliers; raw materials, while having to be imported from abroad, are still readily available; some planning is required for the placement and fulfilment of orders

High risk – Supplies of raw materials can be temporarily unavailable and are always imported from abroad; the price of supplies can fluctuate more than 10%; prices cannot be forecast more than 3 months ahead

Distribution access

Low risk – The ability to access all customers who wish to buy the product or service is easily achieved and without hindrance

Moderate risk – The ability to access all customers who wish to buy the product or service is mixed. Delivery standards are not entirely within the control of the business which may use sub-contractors for delivery

High risk – There are issues regarding accessing all of its customers, delivery is fragmented and the business has limited influence on delivery timescales and schedules

Distribution influence

Low risk – The business has complete control over its entire distribution network and ensures there is consistent uniformity in the standard of its products or services, permitting quality assurances to be provided to its customers

Moderate risk – The business has some control over its distribution network and can exert some influence. It will normally have a mixed range of customers, both direct consumers and wholesalers

High risk – The business has no control over its distribution network, it is characterised by many suppliers, competing with similar products

Distribution elasticity

Low risk – The links in the distribution chain are few and the business has a number of years to plan ahead for any changes or has the ability to respond quickly to changes in consumer habits

Moderate risk – There are a number of links in the distribution chain and generally the business has a limited amount of time to plan ahead for changes; or the business may be hampered economically if there is a sudden change in consumer habits

High risk – There are many links in the distribution chain and at times these can be complicated. Changes occur extremely quickly, consumer habits cannot be forecasted or anticipated

Divisional management performance

- Production performance
- Marketing performance
- Finance performance
- HR performance
- IT performance

Low risk – The division operates consistently to a very high level of efficiency and is held in high regard by its competitors. This also reflects the performance of the manager/director responsible for this area

Moderate risk – The division performs most of the time in an effective, satisfactory and fairly efficient way. This also reflects the performance of the manager/director responsible for this area

High risk – The performance of the division is inconsistent, it is subject to continuous improvement initiatives and its performance is even a drag on the overall business. This also reflects the performance of the manager/director for this area

Number of management/directors

Low risk – All are filled by different individuals

Moderate risk – One individual is responsible for two divisions

High risk – One individual is responsible for three or more divisions

Where managers/directors are responsible for two or more divisions, has key person insurance been provided?

Low risk – Yes, all are covered by full key person insurance for all bank debt levels

Moderate risk – Two are covered by less than 50% key person insurance for agreed bank debt levels

High risk – None are covered by key person insurance

Management/director character

Low risk – All managers/directors are well-established members of the community whose integrity is undoubted

Moderate risk – The management team or directors are all principled individuals who are sound, professional and respected by their workforce and the community

High risk – Opinions have been expressed that the managers/directors do not always act in a respectable and entirely honest manner

Management's/directors' personal credit record

Low risk – Management/directors are known to pay their personal debt punctually or in advance of the due date

Moderate risk – Management/directors are irregular in the payment of their personal debt obligations

High risk – Management/directors are in default of their personal debt obligations

Succession plan

Low risk – The succession plan has been formally prepared and is updated at least biennially

Moderate risk – The succession plan deals with some key issues but does not address adequately. As a result dealing with a change in the management team could adversely affect the business's performance

High risk – Some succession issues have been addressed but the plan is narrow in scope and does not provide fully for the major contingencies such as incapacitation of key leaders. The plan is out of date or no written plan is in place

Employee relations

Low risk – The business has excellent relations with employees, trade unions, etc. Employee opinion surveys reveal high satisfaction rates

Moderate risk – The business has fairly good relations with employees, trade unions, etc. Employee opinion surveys reveal satisfactory satisfaction rates

High risk – The business has poor relations with employees, trade unions, etc. Employee opinion surveys reveal dissatisfaction and employee turnover is higher than the industry norm

Level of environmental risk

Low risk – The business does not produce harmful contaminants in its operations nor does it occupy a property that is situated on contaminated land

Moderate risk – During the manufacturing or production processes, dangerous emissions are released into the factory resulting in contamination or are released into the atmosphere

High risk – During the manufacturing or productions processes, contamination of both the factory and the environment is prevalent

Level of environmental compliance

Low risk – The business fully conforms to all environmental compliance criteria

Moderate risk – The business is in the process of conforming to the required environmental compliance criteria

High risk – The business has not fulfilled its obligations regarding the required environmental compliance criteria

Legal compliance

Low risk – The business is fully compliant with all laws or regulations currently in force

Moderate risk – The business is taking the necessary steps to become compliant with laws that are about to come on to the statute book and is in progress to become fully compliant in the next few months with recent laws or regulations now on the statute book

High risk – The business is not compliant with material regulations or laws

Credit compliance breach

Low risk – Business consistently meets all the terms and conditions of its credit or loan agreement

Moderate risk – Business meets all the major loan covenants but from time to time may fail to comply with minor ones, eg insurance cover has expired, but is being renewed

High risk – Now and then the business breaches a significant term or condition of the credit or loan agreement

Credit covenant breach

Low risk – At this date, no covenants have been breached

Moderate risk – At this date, one covenant has been breached

High risk – At this date two or more covenants have been breached

Business credit reputation

Low risk – Payments to creditors are met before or within agreed terms

Moderate risk – Indications are that payments have extended beyond the agreed terms on an infrequent basis

High risk – Credit checks indicate the business is consistently late, without cause, in paying its suppliers

Business plan success/dealing with catastrophes

Low risk – Both short and long term business plans have been very well executed, resulting in strong business performance

Moderate risk – Implementation of the business plan is generally acceptable. While the business plan addresses normal problems, there is no mention of specific issues. As a result, sometimes the business is unable to achieve forecasted performance

High risk

- No plan – Management has not prepared a formal business plan dealing with the important business and competitive issues
- Plan untested – Although a formal business plan is in place, it has not been tested because the business has only been newly established with no track record or because of a lack of cyclical/competitive experience
- Unsuccessful – Implementation of a business plan has been ineffective causing loss of market position, disruption within the business and financial deterioration

Capital expenditure/technology

Low risk – Production assets, core fixed assets are maintained in a good condition, are regularly maintained, and there is a recognised cycle for replacement. Fixed assets usage percentage under 60%

Moderate risk – Productions assets, core fixed assets are maintained in fairly good order, maintenance is satisfactory, there have been a few breakdowns which have disrupted production and the replacement cycle has not always been adhered to. Fixed assets usage percentage approaching 60% or 66%

High risk – Production assets, core fixed assets are poorly maintained, regular maintenance schedules fall behind, breakdowns happen fairly often disrupting production and the replacement cycle is behind schedule. Fixed assets usage percentage exceeds 66%

In your assessment of financial risk you should be looking at ratings which are moderate and high risks and then differentiate them on three levels:

- Unlikely to happen
- Likely to happen
- Very likely to happen

Requests from customers for credit usually fall within one or more of the seven borrowing requirements; to fund:

- Operating and fixed costs until trade debtors are converted to cash (low risk)
- Stocks until they are converted to output, sales, debtors and then to cash (low risk)
- Property, plant and equipment until they produce output which is converted to sales and then to debtors and then to cash (low risk)
- The whole range of assets required to support rapid growth (low risk)
- A change in the company's ownership (high risk)
- A one-off project, such as property development (high risk)
- Survival until the company can be turned around (very high risk)

When assessing asset and liability risk, the following ratios are used:

- Sales growth percentage
- Gross margin percentage (GM%)
- Operating expenses percentage
- Net margin percentage (NM%)
- Stock days on hand
- Debtor days on hand
- Creditor days on hand
- Capital adequacy percentage
- Gearing percentage
- Interest cover times
- Cash cover percentage

The bank issues a letter confirming the facilities or prepares a loan agreement which the customer signs. The contract will contain such items as:

- The amount
- Period of time covered by the agreement
- The cost of the borrowing
- Repayment terms
- Conditions and covenants
- What the customer needs to do to prevent the facility being withdrawn (in the event of default)
- Security/collateral

Covenants

In essence, the bank is saying to the customer:

- If you maintain items a, b and c of this agreement, we will continue to lend you £x
- Breach these and we will consider this to be an event of default, which allows us to ask for our loan to be repaid immediately or within x days, or seek additional security to protect our increased risk and/or increase the rate of interest

Examples of **conditions precedent** prior to drawdown of increased facilities include:

- If you maintain items a, b and c of this agreement, we will continue to lend you £x
- Breach these and we will consider this to be an event of default, which allows us to ask for our loan to be repaid immediately or within x days, or seek additional security to protect our increased risk and/or increase the rate of interest

Fees will normally be x% of the facility being agreed, with minimum and maximum amounts

Interest rates will be either x% over base rate or over the London Inter Bank Offered Rate (LIBOR)

Each organisation has its own policy on what it requires to charge to meet its internal risk adjusted return on capital – the risk/reward ratio

Notes

8 : Dealing with Financial Difficulties

Topic List

In every lending proposal there is an element of risk. The degree of risk must be carefully evaluated when the proposal is being considered and ultimately the risk must be related to the remuneration (reward) which the bank obtains. However, in recognising that an element of risk is present, we must also accept that things can sometimes go wrong.

Once warning bells have begun to sound, it is essential that you investigate remedial action. It is absolutely wrong to just leave the problem and hope that it will get better and the customer will work through the difficulties!

Danger signs which might indicate that a customer is experiencing problems

From internal bank records

- The customer attempts to take unauthorised excess borrowing
- The customer unexpectedly requests extra borrowing
- The level of turnover (lodgements) through the account is falling
- Evidence of hard core borrowing is emerging
- The customer's cheques are having to be returned unpaid
- Cheques which are lodged by the customer are subsequently returned unpaid
- Cheques for round amounts are being issued by the customer
- The customer regularly issues cheques against uncleared effects
- Cheques issued by the customer are being specially presented
- Numerous status enquiries (opinion requests) are received concerning the customer
- The customer hands to the bank a standing order on favour of a finance company
- Cheques originally lodged by the customer are returned 'payment stopped'
- The customer makes regular significant withdrawals in cash
- Rumours regarding the financial standing/stability of the customer

From interviews/visits to customers

- Staff industry levels/attitudes
- State of repair/age of buildings and machinery
- Machinery not being used to capacity or evidence that is being sold off
- Obsolete stock or overstocking etc

From financial information

- Other borrowings may be revealed
- The figures in the audited accounts may be markedly different from those in the management accounts
- Operating losses may be evident
- Production of financial information and accounts is late
- A change of auditor or an unusual audit fee
- The auditor's statement accompanying the accounts is qualified
- Management accounts are sketchy or non-existent
- The business may be losing valued customers

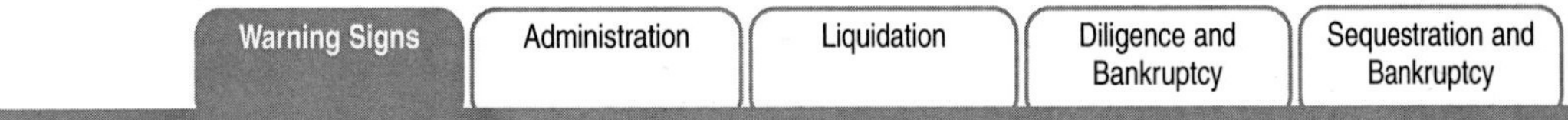

Remedial action by the customer

- Stock
- Debtors
- Creditors
- Other assets
- Other areas for review

Stock: Reducing prices in order to sell off dead or obsolete stock; cutting down on reordering; concentrating on fewer items which are known to be saleable; considering alternative suppliers

Debtors: Are debtors being collected strictly in accordance with agreed terms?

Creditors: In rare instances you may find cash flow difficulties are attributable to creditors being paid prematurely

Other assets: The customer should consider whether any assets are surplus to requirements and could be sold

Other areas for review: Staff costs – cutback through say, a reduction in working hours or a recruitment embargo; capital expenditure – can planned expenditure be postponed or altered?

Purposes of administration

Primary objective is to rescue the company as a going concern; but the administrator can pursue the **secondary objective.** This is done if the primary objective is not reasonably practicable or if the secondary objective would achieve a better result for the company's creditors as a whole

The **third objective** applies only if neither of the first two objectives is possible. It is to realise property/assets in order to make a distribution to one or more secured or preferential creditors, but without 'unnecessarily harming' the interests of the unsecured creditors

Routes into administration

- Court route
- Out of court route

The administrator can run the company in place of the directors, and:

- Raise money by borrowing
- Grant security
- Establish subsidiaries
- Rank and claim in the bankruptcy or whatever of any persons or companies indebted to the company

Invalidity of floating charges

A floating charge can be challenged on the grounds of:

- A gratuitous alienation
- An unfair preference

Other grounds for challenging a floating charge are:

- A floating charge created within a 'relevant time' is invalid, except to the extent of the following, which may be added together:
  - What consists of money paid, or goods or services supplied to the company at the time or after the creation of the charge (this is called *nova debita* – new debt)
  - The value of other debts that were repaid from funds made available because of the creation of the charge
  - The interest which accrued on the account because of the above.
- A charge is considered as having been created within the relevant time in respect of the following:
  - When the charge was created in favour of a person who is connected with the company; the charge was created within a period of two years prior to winding-up beginning; or on presentation of the petition for an administration order
  - Where the charge is issued in favour of any other party, like the bank
  - It had been created within the period of twelve months prior to the commencement of a winding-up or the presentation of a petition for an administration order

Liquidation is the process by which a limited company is terminated

A company may have its existence terminated in one of the following ways:

- Wound up – where the liquidator is a licensed insolvency practitioner
- Struck off the Register of Companies as being defunct
- Dissolved by an order of the court, without being wound up, to enable reconstruction or amalgamation

Compulsory winding-up

One of the most common grounds for winding-up is that the company is 'unable to pay its debts'

- A creditor for a sum exceeding £750 has served on the company a written demand for payment
- The court is satisfied that the company is unable to pay its debts as they fall due
- The court is satisfied that the value of the company's assets is less than the amount of its liabilities

Voluntary winding-up

- Members' voluntary winding-up
- Creditors' voluntary winding-up

The difference between the two is that in a members' voluntary winding-up the directors must be able to make a declaration of solvency

In any winding-up, the liquidator has the following powers

- To sell any of the company's property
- To do all acts executed on behalf of the company
- To prove, rank and claim in the bankruptcy, insolvency or sequestration of any contributory
- To draw, accept, make and endorse any bills of exchange, etc in name of and on behalf of the company
- To raise on the security of the assets of the company any money required
- To take such action in his official name as will be necessary for obtaining payment of any money due from a contributory or his estate which cannot conveniently be done in the name of the company
- To appoint an agent to carry on the business
- To do all such things as will be necessary for the winding-up of the company's affairs and the distribution of its assets

Distribution of assets under liquidation (in strict order)

- The expenses of the liquidation
- Any preferential debts
- Accrued debts
- Ordinary debts
- Interest at the 'official rate' on the first two above from the commencement of winding-up to date of payment
- Any postponed debt

Any surplus remaining is then distributed amongst the members *pro rata*

The Enterprise Act 2002 reformed laws on individual and company insolvency. This Act covers both jurisdictions

Bankruptcy is a generic term used in the law of Scotland covering several types of insolvency. In England, the term covers the process by which an individual is declared by the courts unable to pay their debts and has their affairs administered by a trustee in bankruptcy with assets realised for the benefit of creditors

Bankers need to understand diligence and the relevant law and practice because

- They are often in the position of arrestee when they hold funds or effects of a customer and an arrestment naming the customer as defender is served on the bank
- Customers may discuss the possibility of using diligence when faced with problems of unsettled accounts
- They may require to use diligence where a customer defaults in repayment of an advance

Two types of property against which diligence may be used:

1. Diligence against moveables
2. Diligence against heritable property

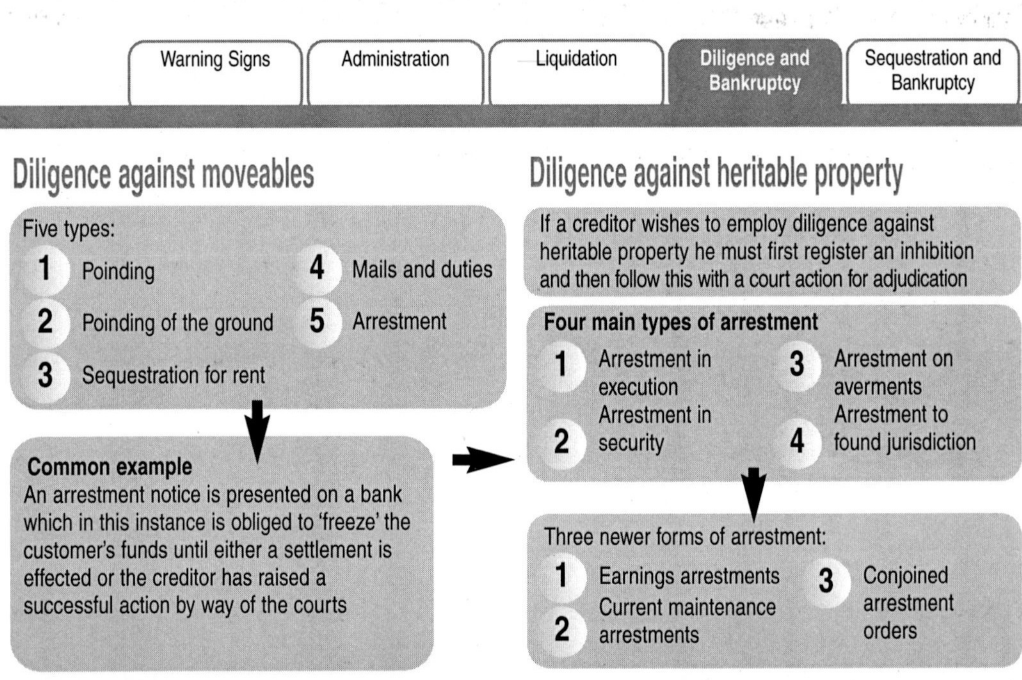

Warning Signs
Administration
Liquidation
Diligence and Bankruptcy
Sequestration and Bankruptcy
Diligence against moveables
Five types:
1 Poinding
2 Poinding of the ground
3 Sequestration for rent
4 Mails and duties
5 Arrestment
Common example
An arrestment notice is presented on a bank which in this instance is obliged to 'freeze' the customer's funds until either a settlement is effected or the creditor has raised a successful action by way of the courts
Diligence against heritable property
If a creditor wishes to employ diligence against heritable property he must first register an inhibition and then follow this with a court action for adjudication
Four main types of arrestment
1 Arrestment in execution
2 Arrestment in security
3 Arrestment on averments
4 Arrestment to found jurisdiction
Three newer forms of arrestment:
1 Earnings arrestments
2 Current maintenance arrestments
3 Conjoined arrestment orders

The procedure at a branch when an arrestment is served

What happens when funds or effects are to be attached?

The customer should be advised that the arrestment has been served together with the effect on the accounts and other items held by the bank

What about the situation where nothing is attached?

If the account is overdrawn and there is no security or right of set-off, there is nothing to attach and in law the customer could continue to lodge funds since these are reducing the debt due to the bank. In practice, the bank would be concerned as the implication is that the customer is not paying debts as they fall due

Enquiries about effects attached

If the arrestment is an arrestment in execution, the bank must reply but care must be exercised and disclosures given should be limited to simply stating whether or not a sum sufficient to meet the debt has been attached. In other cases no information should be given without the consent of the customer

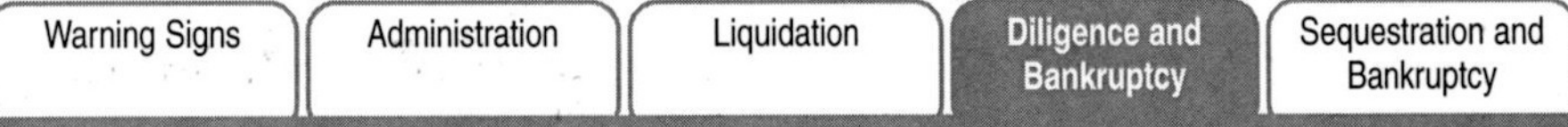

How can the arrestment be loosed?

The defender may obtain an interdict if he can prove malice or oppression.

If the defender pays the debt from some other source or consigns monies to meet it, again the arrestment may be loosed

Further action by the arrester

If none of these things happen, then the arrester has to raise an action of forthcoming

Insolvency

Best described as it was set out in the first *Sale of Goods Act 1893*, which stated that a person is deemed to be insolvent when debts incurred in the ordinary course of business are not paid as they fall due

Types of insolvency:

- Practical insolvency
- Absolute insolvency
- Apparent insolvency

Practical insolvency: This arises where the person's assets, though no less in value than their liabilities, are not available in a sufficiency to meet current debts

Absolute insolvency: The person's liabilities exceed their assets; there is no capital, the consequence is bankruptcy

Apparent insolvency: A debtor appears to be insolvent and the date on which it is established then becomes important in the calendar of subsequent procedures in sequestration

The term 'bankruptcy' has no precise meaning in Scots law. It is sometimes used loosely to mean 'apparent insolvency' but more often in Scotland it is referring to 'sequestration' which is the judicial process where the courts in Scotland decree that the debtor is bankrupt

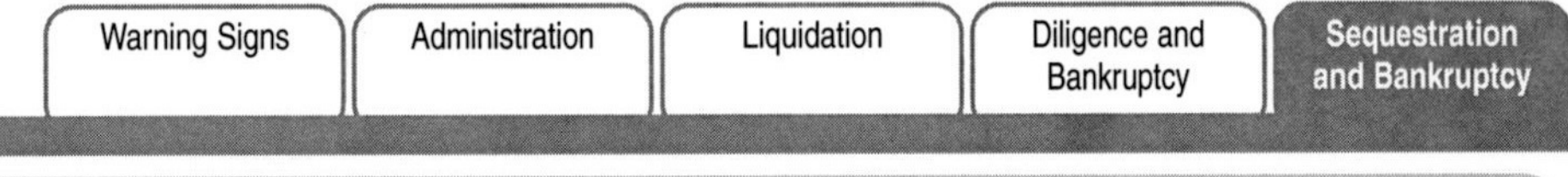

Sequestration is the process whereby an insolvent person is divested of their estate which is then vested in a trustee for the benefit of the creditors

Main stages in full sequestration procedure

- Establish apparent insolvency
- Creditors or the debtor petition the court for award of sequestration
- Advert in the Gazette and entry made in register of inhibitions and adjudication
- Interim trustee appointed
- Statutory meeting called
- Permanent trustee appointed
- Ingathering, realisation and distribution of estate to creditors
- Debtor discharged
- Permanent trustee discharged and accounts audited

Powers of the interim trustee:

- He may require the debtor to deliver to him money, valuables or documents relating to the debtor's business and financial affairs
- He may require the debtor to deliver to him any perishable goods and arrange for their sale
- He can require the debtor to complete transactions started but not finished
- He must prepare a valuation of the debtor's property
- He can close down the debtor's business, or, if the court authorises it, he may carry on the business and has power to borrow money to do this and to preserve the debtor's estate

Duties of the permanent trustee

- Dealing with creditors' claims
- Examination of the debtor
- Deciding on gratuitous alienations or unfair preferences
- Effecting the equalisation of diligence

The order of distribution of the debtor's assets

1. Interim trustee's outlays and remuneration
2. Permanent trustee's outlays and remuneration
3. In the case of a deceased debtor, death-bed and funeral expenses
4. Petitioning creditors' expenses
5. Preferred debts
6. Ordinary debts
7. Interest on preferred and ordinary debts
8. Deferred debts

The term sequestration is not used in England and Wales, the term used is bankruptcy

The bankruptcy procedure

- Begins with a petition to the County Court, or in some cases the High Court
- Following the granting of a Bankruptcy Order, the affairs of the debtor are handled by the Official Receiver
- Within 12 weeks of the order, the Official Receiver must call a creditors' meeting to appoint a trustee in bankruptcy
- When the trustee in bankruptcy is appointed, his function is to liquidate the bankrupt's estate for the benefit of the creditors

During this period and for the duration of the bankruptcy, the bankrupt:

- Cannot obtain credit of more than £500 without disclosing their bankruptcy to the lender
- May not carry on a business unless they do so in the name in which they are bankrupt and announce to all those with whom they deal that they are an undischarged bankrupt
- May not be a company director, or be involved in the management of a company unless the court agrees

Notice of every bankruptcy is published in the London Gazette

If a creditor in bankruptcy holds security from a debtor, they have four options in proof

1. Hand over (surrender) the security to the trustee and prove for the whole debt
2. Not prove at all and simply rely on the value of the security to recover the debt
3. Realise the security and prove for a shortfall as an unsecured creditor
4. Value the security and prove for the shortfall

Distribution of assets

(The order that they appear below is the order in which they rank in any distribution)

1. Secured creditors
2. Liquidation costs
3. Preferential creditors
4. Other creditors

Alternatives to personal bankruptcy are an informal (family) arrangement, an administration order and an individual voluntary arrangement (IVA).

In Scotland the alternative is to sign a trust deed.

Notes

Notes

Notes

Notes

Notes

Notes

Notes

Notes

Notes

Notes

Notes

Notes

Notes

Notes

Notes